"I believe that the way people truly ~~change~~ ~~is by~~ ~~beholding the glory of~~ the Lord. This is why I'm exceedingly thankful for Adam Ramsey's book. Chapter by chapter, with biblical depth and pastoral wisdom, he lifts our gaze up to contemplate the majesty of God. You will find both truth and Spirit in this rich work."

Jared C. Wilson, Assistant Professor of
Pastoral Ministry; Author in Residence, Midwestern Baptist
Theological Seminary; Author, *The Imperfect Disciple*

"Adam Ramsey believes that how we think about God should shape how we experience him. I couldn't agree more. This exquisite book is devotional writing in its purest sense, an invitation not just to know the God of the universe more deeply, but to be overcome in the knowing. *Truth on Fire* compels us to bow our hearts, to experience and exhibit the reverence that beholding God yields. Read it to think, and read it to feel. Herein is a feast for head and heart."

Jen Wilkin, Author, *None Like Him, In His Image*
and *Ten Words to Live By*

"Immediately captivating, Adam Ramsey's fine book challenges us not to settle for a faith wholly dependent on sensational spiritual experiences or, in contrast, one which insists on our minds merely being filled with accurate information about God. Eloquently and effectively he argues for a grasp of gospel truth that makes our hearts burn through an ever-increasing knowledge of him."

Terry Virgo, Founder, Newfrontiers

"'Head vs. Heart.' 'Feelings vs. Facts.' 'Mind vs. Emotion.' 'Doctrine vs. Delight.' 'Truth vs. Affection.' Wouldn't it be wonderful if we could replace the 'vs.' with 'and'? In this book, Adam Ramsey has done just that. *Truth on Fire* is an excellent defense of the absolute necessity of a both/and when it comes to our knowledge and experience of God. You need not live in fear that theological depth will quench the Spirit, nor that heartfelt passion will turn you soft on doctrine. Get this book and let Adam show you why. Highly recommended!"

Sam Storms, Ph.D, Lead Pastor of Preaching and Vision, Bridgeway
Church, Oklahoma City, OK

ADAM RAMSEY

TRUTH
on
FIRE

thegoodbook
COMPANY

Truth on Fire
© Adam Ramsey, 2021.

Published by:
The Good Book Company

thegoodbook.com | thegoodbook.co.uk
thegoodbook.com.au | thegoodbook.co.nz | thegoodbook.co.in

ISBN: 9781784986483 | Printed in Turkey

Design by André Parker

To Liberti,
Jesus is with us.
Onward we stumble.

CONTENTS

FOREWORD

by Ray Ortlund

What energizes us for truly Christian living is not good intentions but true beliefs. Our good intentions help, but they come and go. Who among us isn't weak and wobbly? But our beliefs—especially our beliefs about God—as they deepen, are what will get more and more traction within us for positive change. That is why asking deep questions about God and pondering wise answers from the Bible is a power far beyond our own weakness! It's how, by God's grace, fallible people like us really do become living proof that he is there, that he is real, and that he is beautiful.

This new book by Adam Ramsey will help us all toward greater clarity in our beliefs about God and the difference God makes. That is why I respect and welcome this book.

The backstory to my gratitude begins in 1974. That was when I heard Dr. Francis Schaeffer speak at The Lausanne Congress on World Evangelization in Switzerland. I've never forgotten what he said to us that day.

Schaeffer asked the question, *What is the Christian's task in the world today?* And his answer was not evangelism. Evangelism really matters. But as a stand-alone effort, our evangelism can seem canned, like a sales pitch. Our task in the world today requires a larger, fuller, more human total reality—Christians who together stand out clearly for what we believe, and stand out beautifully for how we embody our beliefs. Then something powerful can start happening.

How then can we Christians and our churches become compelling in this generation? Schaeffer proposed two contents and two realities. The two contents are sound doctrine and honest answers to honest questions. The two realities are true spirituality and the beauty of human relationships. When we are saying something worth listening to, and when we are displaying something worth noticing, we become a prophetic presence in the world today.

What we don't need is cool, impressive, slick, proud. What we do need is truth, honesty, reality, beauty. That's what Schaeffer was pleading for. And his counsel has shaped and guided me all these years.

Now along comes Pastor Adam Ramsey, with Liberti Church in Australia, and I rejoice! As an older pastor, I never stop looking for younger pastors who get it. I look and pray for men who understand, who are good at what they do but who see through empty "success"; pastors who long to see what only God can do and who are willing to walk in his truth and his ways. Adam is that kind of pastor. He cares deeply about what we believe about God, and he cares deeply about how our beliefs can put something of God's own glory upon us.

Adam understands how powerful it is when the grandeur of God gets through to us way down deep. As a true vision of God grips our hearts, something wonderful happens. *God himself visits us at that deep level.* When that happens, who needs a canned, mechanical sales talk for Jesus? The living One just becomes visible, and even obvious, in us! He's good at revealing Christ like that. All he's asking of us is that we admit we're not good at showcasing Jesus, so that we stare at him for a change and let our hearts be amazed. Adam's book, *Truth on Fire*, will help us all do that very thing.

Adam, thank you for writing this book. It is an answer to many prayers and longings. Now may God put his hand on this book and on everyone who reads it, with reviving and reforming impact, for his glory and our joy!

RAY ORTLUND
Renewal Ministries
Nashville, Tennessee

Building the Hearth, Lighting the Flame

"The purpose of theology is doxology—
we study in order to praise."
J.I. PACKER

I want the truth that I believe to be on fire in my life.
I'm guessing you do too.

And I'm also guessing there's a chance that this is not where you are as you open up this book. Perhaps you sense a disconnect between your thinking about God and your experience of God? A gap between the life of your mind and the life of your heart?

Maybe you're part of a church that emphasizes solid Bible teaching and the life of the *mind*. You've experienced a number of wonderful Bible-study groups and maybe even discussed systematic theology with friends, but there's a gnawing sense that something is still missing—an incompleteness. The teaching is meaty and solid, so why does your Christianity feel dry? You can articulate biblical answers and you love the truth of them. But it is truth like a treasured photo of a father who lives far away, when what you really long for is one of his hugs. Deep down you wish you could have a greater experience of the God that you have learned so much about. Is it wrong to want more?

Or maybe your background is in churches that emphasize experiencing God and the life of the *heart*. You are present most Sundays and active in a ministry or two, where you really feel a sense of God's presence. But sometimes, you are not sure that you have much biblical scaffolding to support your very real love for Christ. You get the sense that you should know the God you love a bit better, a bit deeper. Is it wrong to want more?

The simple answer to that question is: no. One of the great tragedies of this present generation of Christians has been the divorce between theological and experiential Christianity. On one side, you tend to have churches committed to theological accuracy, knowing the word of God, and holding a high view of the sacraments of baptism and the Lord's Supper. This team is generally known for expository preaching, systematic theology, and dead white guys who've written lots of books. We'll call this team "The Thinkers." On the other side tend to be churches committed to cultivating an experience of God, knowing the Holy Spirit in personal communion, and engaging the emotions through heartfelt corporate worship experiences. This team reveres passion, cultural relevance, and anything that passes the pragmatic test of, "it works." We'll call this team "The Feelers." The Thinkers often view The Feelers as thoughtless, and The Feelers disregard The Thinkers as lifeless. And more often than not, both are completely right.

What if we didn't have to choose between an intelligent faith and a passionate one? After all, a sharp mind with a cold heart is just as big of a fail as a heart radically on fire about nonsense. The life of the mind and the life of the heart shouldn't really need to be reconciled, because they were always meant to be friends. God intends for us to pursue a Christianity that is radically committed to theological clarity in a way that does not diminish the life of the heart but actually intensifies it. That's what this book will help you to do.

MY STORY: DECONSTRUCTION, RECONSTRUCTION

I grew up in experience-driven churches, each of which were soaked with laughter and light-heartedness and a sense of "life." Our services each week were always positive and uplifting. We had prayer meetings late in the night and early in the morning, where the super-devoted among us came together to seek a deeper experience of God. Evangelism was a high priority. Events were well executed. And the emotional impact during corporate worship was often powerful.

But the older I became, the more I began to notice something: the Bible was present but not central. Vital doctrines were actively avoided. At best, the gospel would sometimes make an appearance at the end of a sermon, but it certainly didn't have any real implications for the daily Christian life. Our emotions were engaged, but our minds were neglected, for fear that we'd be guilty of the great sin of "boredom." People had a good time on Sundays, but weren't equipped to navigate suffering or disappointment well, because they had a view of God that didn't line up with reality. And any time a church has a high view of themselves and a low view of God, it becomes a hotbed for hypocrisy. There was no greater place where I saw this than in the mirror.

I began to wrestle with the Scriptures; especially the parts I had never once heard a sermon about. Words like *sovereignty* and *election, propitiation* and *providence* were like signposts in a new country that I was eager to explore. I decided to lay all my cards on the table—everything I thought I knew about God—and push it all through the filter of the Bible to see what would come out the other side. I opened God's word with new appetite. I read the 4th and 5th-century Church Fathers (like Athanasius and Augustine), the 16th-century Reformers (like Martin Luther and John Calvin), and the 17th and 18th-century Puritans (pretty much any guy who wore black and was named John or Thomas). I even engaged in an epic battle of counterpoints and arguments with the (21st-century) preacher John Piper through his books and online sermons—which he of course was completely unaware of, but that he still managed to win. And here's what happened: as my mental image of God increased in magnitude, I discovered that so too did my desire for holiness, my gratitude for grace, my delight in worship, and my boldness in mission.

But something else was also growing during my personal theological reformation. A spiritual weed growing subtly alongside the fruit: pride. An intellectual brashness that delighted in simply being right. Now that I had more of the biblical facts, it became way too easy to settle for having a more accurate understanding of God at the expense of a joy-soaked, moment-by-moment communion with God. Fortunately, my wife along with my pastor both called me out on it while it was still in its infancy. "Knowledge puffs up, but love builds up," said the apostle Paul (1 Corinthians 8:1). By God's grace, I learned the first part of that verse early on in my theological discoveries, even though it would take many more years for the second part to become more evident in my life.

A few years went by, and our family relocated from Australia to Seattle, when I was asked to take on the role of teaching the Bible to young people at a church called Mars Hill. At that point, it was considered one of the fastest-growing churches in the United States, under the teaching ministry of one of the most well-known preachers in the world at that time. The content was biblical and meaty and robust, and thousands were being baptised each year. Yet before the many other problems that were eventually exposed at Mars Hill became obvious—ultimately leading to its collapse—some of the first questions my wife and I were asking about our new theological tribe were: *Why is there such an absence of joy when we gather together in worship? Why do the prayers have no more fervency than a jazz radio-station host pulling the late shift? How come there are so many people who can articulate biblical theology, yet also lament any kind of meaningful intimacy with the God their theology points to?*

THEOLOGY ON FIRE

The first half of my Christian life had engaged my emotions but not my mind. The second half engaged my mind but not my emotions. Having spent time in both of these camps respectively, I had grown tired of the divide. I wanted both. I wanted truth on fire.

And that is exactly what God wants for me, and for you, as well. After all, didn't Jesus say that the most important command in the whole universe was that we cultivate a love for God that includes all our heart *and* all our mind (Mark 12:28-30)?

So why is it that so often we settle for just one or the other? Here's why: we are afraid.

Some of us are afraid of a theologically robust Christianity that engages only our minds, because we've experienced the cold lovelessness from those who prefer arguing over adoring and debating over delighting. We naturally shrink back from those who weaponize theology. Christians who can articulate the doctrines of grace but lack graciousness—who understand the nuances of justification but have lives absent of joy—are, at best, confusing. At worst, they can cause great damage to their brothers and sisters in Christ.

Others of us are afraid of an experiential Christianity that engages only the emotions, because we've seen the damage that takes place when spiritual experience is separated from biblical literacy. We're tired of hyped-up, talk-show Christianity that feels about as authentic as a laugh-track on a 90's sitcom. We've seen the impotency of worshiping worship and having faith in faith. We want the truth, the real thing, the reality of God, as he has revealed himself through his word.

It's time to leave our fears behind by seeing how we can have both—rather than having to choose between—the robust *and* the experiential. If right thinking is the hearth, then right experience is the flame. We need both. Without the hearth, our spiritual experiences can run wild, leaving many burn-victims in their wake. Without the flame, our magnificent theology is cheapened into a nice decoration, sitting pointlessly and lifelessly in the corner of our lives. So we cannot settle for one without the other. The 13th-century preacher Anthony of Padua, who was entrusted with the theological instruction of the followers of Francis of Assisi, began each of his classes with the phrase, "Of what value is learning, that does not turn to love?"[1] Our goal must always be both.

In one of the famous scenes of the popular TV show *Friday Night Lights*, Coach Taylor rallies his high school football team with what becomes the iconic motto of the show: "Clear eyes, full hearts, can't lose." Doesn't this describe the kind of Christianity that deep down we all long for? Isn't this both/and of head *and* heart exactly what Paul prays for when he writes from a prison cell, "And it is my prayer that your *love* may abound more and more, with *knowledge* and all discernment" (Philippians 1:9)? Doesn't Peter say the same thing? "Finally, all of you, have … a tender heart, and a humble mind" (1 Peter 3:8). If this is normal Christianity, why should we settle for anything less? Here's some good news: we don't have to choose between theological precision and white-hot passion. God wants us to reject both dead orthodoxy as well as passionate ignorance.

Clear eyes. Full heart. Can't lose.

Right thinking. Right feeling. That is what we are made for.

Truth that's on fire. That's what this book is all about.

A PATH FORWARD

A.W. Tozer opened his classic work *The Knowledge of the Holy* with the statement: "What comes into our minds when we think about God is the most important thing about us."[2] Every Christian should want to know accurately what the God they love is actually like. In this way, clear theological thinking becomes to me like a photo of my wife: it reveals to me the beauty of the one I love. Sound doctrine matters, because it shows us the qualities of the God we worship. Biblical literacy matters, because as the author Jen Wilkin reminds us, "The heart cannot love, what the mind does not know."[3] Each chapter of this book will focus on a specific attribute or quality of God. Section 1 of this book will focus on some of God's *incommunicable attributes*, that is, those things that are true about him (such as his transcendence and omnipotence) that are only true about *him*. Section 2 zeroes in on some of God's *communicable attributes*, which are the characteristics of God that can also be increasingly reflected in our own lives (such as love, gentleness, and happiness), as we walk with Jesus.

Along with highlighting the various attributes of God, we will also see how these attributes are personified in Jesus Christ. If Jesus truly is "the radiance of the glory of God and the exact imprint of his nature" (Hebrews 1:3), then we can expect the attributes of God to be sharpened into high-resolution quality in the life of Jesus. Jesus is not a blurred photocopy of what God is like. He is *exactly* what God is like. So that which might be obscure to us about the nature of God, Jesus brings into focus. We can learn what God is like by getting to know what Jesus, the God-Man, is like.

Finally, our end goal is to not merely fill our minds with true knowledge about God (as important as that is), but for that knowledge to reshape our hearts and experience of God in our daily lives. That's why each chapter ends with a handful of questions that can be used for personal reflection or discussion in groups. Good theology matters, but it's not our final destination. It exists to move us into a deeper experience of the one for whom we have been created. It is the rocket-fuel of our worship.

Imagine if an intelligent faith and a passionate faith were both realities in your discipleship to Jesus. Imagine churches that were known for both a high view of the Holy Scriptures as well as a high view of the Holy Spirit (*who, you know, wrote them*).

My hope in these pages is to paint a biblical portrait of what God is *actually* like, so that we can gaze upon him together until our hearts can't help but sing. To behold him in such a way that our daily experience is transformed with a deepened awareness of who it is we pray to, who it is that is with us, and who it is that we are loved by. To think about our God more deeply, in order to enjoy him more intensely. To let God's truth set our hearts on fire.

CHAPTER 1

God is Other:
The Experience of Wonder

*"Ultimately, when it comes to God, we're like ants crawling
across an iPad: in touch with something we only
faintly understand."*
DREW DYCK

It was late afternoon, and after ten days of preaching in
rural Zambia, five of us were squeezed onto a small boat
gliding quietly across shallow water toward the riverbank.
We had hoped to catch a glimpse of some local wildlife, but
we weren't expecting this: directly in front of us stood a full-
grown African elephant, hiding behind some thin trees about
as conspicuously as a Vegas billboard in an Amish settlement.
Our guide turned off the motor, and a nervous silence settled
over the group as the tide inched us closer. We sat motionless,
hardly daring to breathe, just metres away from untamed
power that had never known a master. We were in awe.

Suddenly, the thin trees separating us from the elephant
crackled then bowed forward as this heavyweight champion
of Africa pressed over them into the shallow water directly
toward us. A few more steps and he would have joined us
in the boat. Everyone gasped. A pastor swore. The guide
quickly throttled backward to a safer distance, and we looked
at one another with racing hearts and astonished faces that

all preached the same one-word sermon: *wonder.* We spent the entire trip back upriver shot with adrenaline, shaking our heads, laughing that unique species of laughter that appears only when you've come face to face with your own mortality.

Wonder. It is something easier experienced than explained, for the description never quite does justice to the reality. But it's a reality we all have bumped into at one time or another through the course of our lives. We might compare it to an internal explosion, brought about by beholding external greatness. Delight and surprise and curiosity and sometimes even terror all mix together to remind us how wonderfully small and creaturely we really are. Like standing in the presence of a wild elephant. Or the first time we tasted chocolate. Or an unexpected kiss on our teenage lips. Or catching a glimpse of a meteor shower.

And in a very real way, that same feeling of awe is meant to mark our walk with Jesus. Real worship is undergirded by a perpetual sense of wonder as we fix our eyes on the God who is unparalleled in beauty and unrivalled in power.

GOD IS OTHER

If you're anything like me, "wonder" is not the first word that comes to mind when you consider your own Christianity. All too often, our experience of prayer, the Bible, and church can be, well, underwhelming. The problem, as the 16th-century Reformer Martin Luther once quipped to his theological rival Erasmus, is that "your thoughts of God are too human." Tamed views of the Divine are almost always the result of a "God-in-the-mirror" theology, where we see the Lord of all as little more than a reflection of ourselves; a God who conveniently winks at almost everything we presently practice and approve of, rarely being so audacious as to contradict our wishes.

But that is not the picture of God we find in Scripture. That God—as he truly is—will not allow us to catch him, cage him, and comprehensively examine him like a neat little specimen. We need to first appreciate the otherworldly dissimilarity between us and the God who beckons, "Seek my face" (Psalm 27:8).

There's a scene in C.S. Lewis's *The Silver Chair*, where Jill, a self-assured newcomer to the land of Narnia, has been separated from her friend Eustace, and is searching for a stream to satisfy her raging thirst. She follows the sounds of flowing water and finally locates this source of life, but upon arrival she stops dead in her tracks. For next to the stream stands the one who sang Narnia into existence: Aslan the Lion. Paralysed with uncertainty as to whether she ought to approach or flee for her life, she is surprised when the Great Lion opens his mouth and speaks to her:

"Are you not thirsty?" said the Lion.

"I am dying of thirst," said Jill.

"Then drink," said the Lion.

"May I—could I—would you mind going away while I do?" said Jill.

The Lion answered this only by a look and a very low growl. And as Jill gazed at its motionless bulk, she realised that she might as well have asked the whole mountain to move aside for her convenience. The delicious rippling noise of the stream was driving her nearly frantic.

"Will you promise not to—do anything to me, if I do come?" said Jill.

"I make no promise," said the Lion.

Jill was so thirsty now that, without noticing it, she had come a step nearer.

"Do you eat girls?" she said.

"I have swallowed up girls and boys, women and men, kings and emperors, cities and realms," said the Lion. It didn't say this as if it were boasting, nor as if it were sorry, nor as if it were angry. It just said it.

"I daren't come and drink," said Jill.

"Then you will die of thirst," said the Lion.

"Oh dear!" said Jill, coming another step nearer. "I suppose I must go and look for another stream then."

"There is no other stream," said the Lion.[4]

Like Lewis's Lion, God will not be tamed. He offers fullness of life, but he does so on *his* terms. Yet we must approach him. *For there is no other stream.*

Throughout Scripture, we are confronted with a God who is entirely other to us. A God who questions us, "To whom then will you compare me, that I should be like him?" (Isaiah 40:25) and corrects us, "You thought I was one like yourself" (Psalm 50:21). To be sure, there is a profound sense in which we *are* like God (which we'll talk about in chapter 10); yet in a deeper way, God is entirely *unlike* us. The theological attribute we are talking about here is called the transcendence of God. Or put another way, the "Godness" of God. God reminds us of just how other his "otherness" is through the prophet Isaiah:

> *Remember what happened long ago, for I am God, and there is no other; **I am God, and no one is like me.** I declare the end from the beginning, and from long ago what is not yet done, saying: my plan will take place, and I will do all my will. (Isaiah 46:9-10, CSB)*

Who among us can say that? Who among us not only *knows* the beginning and the end of all things, but *declares* them?

Who among us can say that our every plan has come to fruition? No one. There is no one like him.

What makes the gap of God's transcendence so insurmountable is that, biblically speaking, God does not merely exist in the highest possible category; he goes beyond the concept of categories. He *creates* the categories. To borrow the imagery of Tozer, God is not merely at the top of the list of beings that descend downward in gloriousness from him: God, angels, humans, mammals, reptiles, insects, bacteria… cats. (*Ok fine, Tozer said "caterpillars" but who's to say autocorrect hasn't been a problem for generations?*) The point is: God is not even on the list. He transcends the list. He made the list. Tozer writes that God is…

> … as high above an archangel as above a caterpillar, for the gulf that separates the archangel from the caterpillar is but finite, while the gulf between God and the archangel is infinite. The caterpillar and the archangel, though far removed from each other in the scale of created things, are nevertheless one in that they are alike created. They both belong in the category of that-which-is-not-God and are separated from God by infinitude itself.[5]

SELF-EXISTING AND UNCHANGING

Not only is God different to us in the *category* of his being but in the *essence* of his being. How so? He needs nothing outside of himself to exist, and in his self-existence, he does not shift a single millimetre away from perfection. He is the "living God and the everlasting King" (Jeremiah 10:10), who is the "only Sovereign, the King of kings and Lord of lords, who alone has immortality" (1 Timothy 6:16). Theologians call this the aseity—or self-existence—of God.

Think of it like this. *We* are needy. *We* are very fragile. To live, we are completely dependent on sustenance, water, and an environment within a very narrow window of survivable temperatures. And I haven't even mentioned the unconscious, ongoing expression of dependency known as *breathing* that you've been silently leaning on without realising it since you opened this book. But God needs nothing outside of himself to exist. No oxygen is required, no preconditioned environment is necessary; nothing is depended on outside of himself. He is, in himself, all that is needed; happy and whole. Everything else that exists—from exploding supernovas down to cellular mitosis—only does so because *he* does.

On top of that, he does not change. God is immutable. He always acts like himself; that is to say, he is not evolving or improving. Neither his essence nor his character changes. He is "the Father of lights, with whom there is no variation or shadow due to change" (James 1:17). While we can be radically altered in our personality through a single tragedy or profoundly change our beliefs the moment our circumstances no longer line up with our plans, God's purposes and God's word remain steadfast. We are ever-changing, he is never-changing. When Moses asked his name, God replied to him not with a label, but with a statement of his unchanging existence: "I AM WHO I AM (Exodus 3:14). That is God's way of saying to us, *There was never a time I was not, and there will never be a time where I will be not.* He simply and gloriously, is.

JESUS: THE 'I AM' ON DISPLAY

Have you noticed that, in the Gospels, when people encountered Jesus as he truly was, they never responded with a shrug of indifference? People wondered at him and worshiped him, or they picked up rocks to stone him. They either went great lengths to be near him or to rid the world of him.

When some religious leaders challenged Jesus as to who he really was, he responded with the same declaration of eternal, self-existence that God gave to Moses: "Truly, truly, I say to you, before Abraham was, I am" (John 8:58). He deliberately applied the unchanging otherness of God, to himself. Another time Jesus revealed his otherworldliness was in Mark 4, where, after spending the day teaching large crowds beside the sea, Jesus decided it was time for him and his disciples to cross to the other side.

> *And a great windstorm arose, and the waves were breaking into the boat, so that the boat was already filling. But he was in the stern, asleep on the cushion. And they woke him and said to him, "Teacher, do you not care that we are perishing?" And he awoke and rebuked the wind and said to the sea, "Peace! Be still!" And the wind ceased, and there was a great calm. (Mark 4:37-39)*

Here was a storm so fierce that even the experienced fishermen of Jesus' crew, who had grown up on the sea, were terrified for their lives. Jesus woke from his nap, looked at the raging storm, and spoke three words, "Peace! Be still!" Actually in the Hebrew, it's only two words. A pair of verbs, that could loosely translate into English, "Sit down, stay down." And the hurricane immediately obeyed him. This was no magic trick or incantation or appeal to a higher power for help. This was Jesus, "the Word [who] became flesh and dwelt among us" (John 1:14)—the one through whom all creation came into being (v 1-3)—speaking to a storm with an authority that belonged only to the Creator himself.

The angry waves and tantrumming winds recognised the ancient voice that called them into existence at the very beginning, and sat obediently at their Master's feet. Christ spoke. Creation listened. And the disciples trembled:

> *He said to them, "Why are you so afraid? Have you still no faith?" And they were filled with great fear and said to one*

another, "Who then is this, that even the wind and the sea obey him?" (Mark 4:40-41)

Why were those who knew and walked with Jesus more afraid after the storm than during it? Why didn't calm enter their hearts, when it entered their surroundings? Here's why: in that moment, the disciples realised that they had better odds of taming the power outside the boat than taming the one who was inside their boat. Yet the one who was infinitely above them, was also right there, intimately with them. No wonder they trembled with wonder.

MATURING TOWARD CHILDLIKENESS

By this point, our jaw might be slightly agape in reverence of God, but the shape of our mouth may not yet be that of a smile. Let's press a little deeper. The type of wonder Jesus calls us to is childlikeness. I'm sure there are many reasons Jesus said, "Unless you turn and become like children, you will never enter the kingdom of heaven" (Matthew 18:3). But surely one of them had to do with a child's capacity for experiencing amazement? In fact, Jesus seemed to have a standard response for his followers when they began drifting toward an inflated view of themselves. He'd point them to a little child.

To a child, worshipful wonder is natural. Children possess a delightful curiosity that causes them to run toward that which astonishes them, rather than shrink back from it or simply shrug it off. The world around them is bursting with newness to be admired, whether it's a butterfly in the garden, a pretty pebble in the dirt, a ride in the front seat of the car, or a song from a Frozen movie playing for the ten billionth time: all seem to elicit a "wow" from their smiling little mouths. When it comes to awe, children are the experts.

And yet, it is this capacity to truly wonder that is often one of the first casualties of growing up. As we become more routined and "used to" life in this world, we seem to become less surprisable. More cynical. And more numb to glory, even when it's right under our noses.

What if a childlike curiosity and wonder and openness were to mark our living, rather than a settled sense of self-assurance? It may seem counterintuitive, but Christian growth is a gradual downward movement toward the maturity of childlikeness. Have you ever met a Christian in their later years whose eyes sparkled bright with life? That is a person growing toward childlikeness of heart, not away from it. When we find ourselves in a season of life that seems dry and predictable, when we open God's word with a casual sense of familiarity, when we pray like we're approaching a customer service agent instead of a loving Father, it's worth asking ourselves, "Have I been moving away from childlikeness instead of maturing into childlikeness? Have I become too grown up for my own good?"

A HERMENEUTIC OF ADORATION

We need only open our eyes to the signposts of God's glory all around us that our self-absorption has blinded us to. God has graciously given us a world to inhabit that is dripping with his creative majesty, reminding us that we are standing in a story that is much, much bigger than ourselves. And he reveals a picture of himself to us in his word that is anything but dull. The late pastor Eugene Peterson called this "cultivating a hermeneutic of adoration." A hermeneutic is simply our way of reading the Bible. Adoration means deep and worshipful love. Putting these two words together, Peterson encourages us to read God's world and God's word hand in hand:

> Look at the world with childlike wonder, ready to be startled into surprised delight by the profuse abundance of truth and beauty and goodness that is spilling out

of the skies at every moment ... And then practice
this hermeneutic of adoration in the reading of Holy
Scripture. Plan on spending the rest of your lives
exploring and enjoying the world both vast and intricate
that is revealed by this text.[6]

My heart remembers how to adore when I slow down long enough in the rush of 21st-century life to earnestly gaze upon the creative genius of God. A late summer-night sunset in the Isle of Skye, alive with unspeakable purples and reds; the delicious sounds of a crackling fire; the existence of coffee; the way water can float softly in the delicate form of a snowflake or crash with thundering symmetry in a wave at Teahupo'o; the stillness of dawn; the smell of Australian rain; the ridiculousness of llamas; the laughter of a daughter. If I pay attention to God's world, I am assaulted with delight.

And when I stare into God's word, I am reminded that he who created all the beauty I just described is the same one who spans the universe with his hand (Isaiah 40:12); who calls forth all of the trillions of galaxies, that each contain hundreds of billions of stars, which he knows all by name (Psalm 147:4). Stars like VY Canis Majoris, which is big enough to swallow up a few quadrillion earths and still have room for dessert. The Scriptures point to a God of unmatchable wisdom, unlimited riches, and unsearchable judgments (Romans 11:33). There is a greater likelihood of a bulldog mastering Bach or a cactus grasping quantum theory than there is of you and I plumbing the depths of the Divine, in this life or eternity. Nobody who catches even the faintest glimpse of this God walks up to him with a swagger or away from him with a yawn.

So go ahead and stare dumbstruck for a while at the magnificent otherness of God on display in his world and his word. Don't worry about how small it makes you feel. Embrace it. For small is what you are. Behold your creaturely dependence, and then raise your eyes as high as you can strain them to the heights of God's uncreated permanence. In that place, grownups are again made childlike, and the life-weary are renewed with wonder.

Are you thirsty? Do you feel dry with God? He invites you to come and drink. But remember, you must receive him as he is. He will not be managed any more than a Galilean thunderstorm or a Narnian Lion.

Remember that God is *God*.

Remember that God is *other*.

Remember that God *is*.

REFLECTING AND APPLYING

1. What are some ways the otherness of God revealed in Scripture thrills your heart?

2. What are some ways that God's otherness makes your heart tremble?

3. Think on Jesus' words about childlikeness. Where in your Christianity have you lost a sense of wonder, and perhaps become too grown-up for your own good?

4. When you slow down to stare at God's world, what do you see around you that fills you with a sense of awe?

CHAPTER 2

God is Sovereign: The Experience of Assurance

"Christianity is not about what we can do; it's about what God promises to do for us. Christianity is not fundamentally challenge; fundamentally it is assurance."

RAY ORTLUND

Among the most inspiring women of the 20th century was a watchmaker's daughter in the Netherlands named Corrie ten Boom. In her book *The Hiding Place*, Corrie tells of how her family sheltered hundreds of Jews during the Second World War from the murderous pursuits of the Nazis. Eventually their home was raided, and the ten Boom family were marched away into Hitler's infamous concentration camps.

Corrie and her sister Betsie eventually found themselves in the Ravensbrück concentration camp over the German border. By that time, the barracks that were built for 250 women were housing 1,500-2,000, with five to a bed and many more on the straw-matted floor. Corrie and Betsie were marched to Barracks 28, a dilapidated structure with broken windows, soiled bedding, backed-up plumbing, and bad-tempered guards. And to top it off, Barracks 28 was infested with biting fleas. *Really God? As if things weren't bad enough already?*

Over the coming weeks, the sisters began ministering in the miserable conditions of Barracks 28 to the other women around them; praying with them, encouraging one another, and reading from a small Bible they had smuggled in. Though the guards were all within earshot, they rarely entered the barracks, which created more opportunities for the sisters to speak of Jesus to the others. They soon discovered why. Corrie writes:

> One evening I got back to the barracks late. … Betsie was waiting for me, as always, so that we could wait through the food line together. Her eyes were twinkling.
>
> "You're looking extraordinarily pleased with yourself," I told her.
>
> "You know, we've never understood why we had so much freedom in the big room," she said. "Well—I've found out."
>
> That afternoon, she said, there'd been confusion in her knitting group about sock sizes and they'd asked the supervisor to come and settle it. But she wouldn't. She wouldn't step through the door and neither would the guards. And you know why?
>
> Betsie could not keep the triumph from her voice: "Because of the fleas! That's what she said, 'That place is crawling with fleas!'"[7]

Why did these two sisters have the freedom to provide hope and help in the darkest of circumstances?

Because in the sovereign hands of God, the fleas controlled the Nazis.[8] If God is sovereign, we can finally rest from pretending that *we* are. And if we believe that Christ is on the throne, we too can live with assurance, even in the most difficult of circumstances.

WHO IS IN CHARGE HERE?

To be sovereign means to be ultimate in authority, and the key is found in the last five letters: *reign*. When we talk about sovereignty, we are exploring the question of *Who is in charge here?* If life is a story, who is holding the pen? Who is the one deciding things—from the cosmic level of the location of each star, down to the comical level of the shapes of human toes?

The Scriptures remind us that we are not in the hands of fate, chaos, devils, demons, or even ourselves, but in the secure hands of an infinitely sovereign and infinitely good God who is powerfully at work in everything for his glory. Sovereignty, when wed to the limitless transcendence of God, does not merely mean "best"; it means unbeatable. Peerless. Unparalleled. The God-of-the-throne reigns with total supremacy; a reign described by A.W. Pink as, "unrivalled in majesty, unlimited in power, unaffected by anything outside himself."[9] He is wonderfully unworried by any potential challenger to his crown.

The biblical authors paint a picture of the God Most High who alone holds the deed to the heavens and the earth (Genesis 14:19), whose dominion will endure through all generations until the very end of time as we understand it (Psalm 145:13). Imagine a circle, in the middle of which are written the words "all created things." According to Isaiah, God holds that sphere of "all created things" in his hand, with the ease that Michael Jordan palms a basketball (Isaiah 40:12). Here is a God who stands sovereign over creation (Psalm 146:6; Romans 11:36); sovereign in salvation (John 6:37, 44; Romans 8:29-30; 9:15-16); sovereign over all things (Romans 8:28), forcing even evil and suffering to bend backward on themselves and accomplish his purposes, without himself ever being the author of evil (Genesis 50:20; James 1:13). He can do what he wants, wherever he wants, whenever he wants, for as long as he wants.

It's important that we understand that the extent of God's sovereignty extends over not only the nice and happy and pleasing things, but over *all* things. Even the painful things. *Especially* the painful things. For it is in our pain—from the smaller irritations of life like fleas to the perplexing existence of evils like Nazis—that we most need the anxiety-incinerating comfort that can only be provided by a God on the throne. Think about it: if even one thing falls outside the scope of God's sovereignty, how will we ever be able to rest in the assurance that *God really has got this*? Instead, Christians can live with the confidence that not one moment of suffering in their lives will ever be wasted. Under God's sovereign foot, every beating we experience in this life will be trodden into the fine wine of a Christlike life. At the end of this age we will look back and see how—in God's hands—even our sufferings were turned into servants of our sanctification (we'll explore this more in chapter 6).

After writing of this God's great and sovereign grace for eleven straight chapters in the book of Romans, it's no wonder Paul suddenly bursts into song:

> *Oh, the depth of the riches and wisdom and knowledge of God! How unsearchable are his judgments and how inscrutable his ways! "For who has known the mind of the Lord, or who has been his counsellor?" "Or who has given a gift to him that he might be repaid?" For from him and through him and to him are all things. To him be glory for ever. Amen. (Romans 11:33-36)*

His ways are "inscrutable" (v 33)—there is no governing board that he seeks approval from. No one has been his counsellor (v 34)—he has no up-line, no commanding officer, no checks and balances, and he will never be in our debt. There are no limits to his authority. He is the King of kings and the Lord of lords, who exists in a category all of his own, which no one can even come close to. Even his apparent "wrong moves" still lead to an inevitable checkmate of all who oppose him. Who among us can say with God: *No one has ever taught me, disciplined me, corrected me, counselled me, enriched me, measured me, or improved me* (Isaiah 40:12-14; Romans 11:33-36)?

In other words, God is even more *Godlike* than you think. Nothing is so big that it intimidates him, or so small that it escapes his attention. He is as sovereign over the difficulties awaiting you next Tuesday, as he is the renewal of the universe.

JESUS SOVEREIGN OVER HIS CREATION

As we've already seen, Jesus flexed his sovereignty in his command over the created world. At the sound of his word, storms sat quietly at their Maker's feet (Mark 4:35-41); fig trees withered up and were no more (Matthew 21:18-21); ordinary water was upgraded into the finest of red wines (John 2:1-11)—or as the 17th-century poet Richard Crashaw described it, "The conscious water saw its Creator, and blushed."

If Jesus ruled with sovereign ease over the elements when he walked this world, how much more so does the risen and exalted Jesus reign while seated on his throne? Not a molecule of the universe exists outside the scope of his sovereign authority, as Paul reminds the Colossians:

> *By him all things were created, in heaven and on earth, visible and invisible, whether thrones or dominions or rulers or authorities—all things were created through him and for him. And he is before all things, and in him all things hold together. (Colossians 1:16-17)*

Christ looks at everything that exists as being within the borders of his kind and kingly dominion. As the Dutch theologian Abraham Kuyper famously declared, "There is not a square inch in the whole domain of our human existence over which Christ, who is Sovereign over all, does not cry: 'Mine!'"[10]

JESUS SOVEREIGN OVER HIS MISSION

Not only is Jesus sovereign over all of creation, he also reigns over the great plan of redemption to save a people for his own possession (1 Peter 2:9-10). Immediately before Jesus commissioned the disciples to the seemingly insurmountable mission of making disciples through the entire world, he wanted them to be assured of one thing: he is totally and completely in charge.

> *And Jesus came and said to them, "All authority in heaven and on earth has been given to me. Go therefore and make disciples of all nations..." (Matthew 28:18-19)*

Think of how nervous we can feel just crossing the room to share the gospel with someone who doesn't know Christ yet. Then imagine how impossible this commission would have felt to the disciples! Why was it so important to Jesus, that he front-load the mission with this reminder of his sovereignty? Because Jesus wants us to remember that though he has graciously included *us* in God's mission, he has not abdicated ultimate responsibility for this mission. How could it be otherwise? And if it were otherwise, how could we even get out of bed tomorrow morning and attempt to live faithfully for his glory with any hope of success?

We'd end up feeling like Sisyphus, the ancient king of Corinth from Greek mythology who was condemned by the gods to an eternity of pointlessness. Each day, he would push an enormous boulder to the top of one of hell's hills. As he would near the summit, the weight of the boulder would roll back on him, sending him tumbling down the mountain, and he would begin his impossible task again. Unending futility. Unceasing struggle. An unachievable mission.

Remove Christ's sovereignty from the Great Commission, and we are all Sisyphus. It won't be long before we find ourselves overwhelmed by the size of the mountain before us and eventually crushed by a weight that our creaturely frames were never designed to bear. But the sovereignty of Christ, who "upholds the universe by the word of his power" (Hebrews 1:3), is rocket fuel for following him onto his mission with assurance!

Jesus is on the throne and no one can vote him off. Therefore, you can share the gospel with assurance, confident that even in the face of rejection or hostility, Christ is on the throne and changes hearts in his own time through your faithful witness.

Jesus is the Lord of lords, and no committee can fire him. Therefore, you can stand firm, even as our culture shifts and changes; you don't need to be afraid of being caught on "the wrong side of history" because you stand upon the rock of God's word that will outlast the entire world.

Jesus is the King of kings, and no power of man or army of hell can overthrow him. Therefore, you can pray for loved ones with renewed confidence, because the God who has given you access to his throne also loves to hear your voice (Hebrews 4:16; Ephesians 2:18).

If Jesus is sovereign, we can lay our hearts to rest, even as we busily get to work.

REST FOR RECOVERING CONTROL FREAKS

To those of us who've grown up breathing the 21st-century air of autonomy and individualism so prevalent within Western cultures, the realisation of God's sovereignty can feel like coming into contact with a right hook from Mike Tyson. We spend our lives drawing assurance from our ability to control things (or convincing ourselves that we can). We don't like to acknowledge our helplessness. But whether it is the dependent cry of a newborn, the heartbreak of relational betrayal in our teens, the welcome-to-reality moment of our twenties, the crisis of purpose in our middle years, or the slow acceptance of mortality that comes near the dusk of our days, the sharp edges of life have a way of bursting the illusion we have made for ourselves, that at some level, "I am in charge here."

Every Christian, to some degree, is a recovering control freak. It is only when we come to the place of accepting our rightful role as creature rather than Creator, servant rather than Master, child rather than Father, that we find the rest we most long for.

So ask yourself: *How does Jesus reigning on the throne make me feel? Does it unsettle me or does it comfort me?* While it's unlikely I'd ever say it so bluntly, the truth is that I will only be unsettled by God's sovereignty if, deep down, I think that he cannot be trusted with such authority. Or that I could do a better job. The first reveals a heart that doesn't yet know him as he has revealed himself; the second is how the devil became the devil. God being on the throne only threatens me to the degree that my flesh is planning a coup.

Here's what happens when we really understand the doctrine of God's sovereignty: his occupation of the throne no longer terrifies us. To the contrary, it satisfies us, like a pillow for a weary head. It refreshes us like a desert oasis to a weary traveller. God's throne is only repulsive to the rebellious heart. For his children, it is a throne of grace which we now approach with confidence to "receive mercy and find grace to help in time of need" (Hebrews 4:16). And the more certain we become of this—that God is sovereign over all things—the more assurance we'll have to follow him into anything, and trust him with everything.

IMMORTAL TILL HIS WORK IS DONE
In 1866, when John Paton arrived with his family to the New Hebrides in the South Pacific (now Vanuatu), he was

setting up his home among a people with a reputation for cannibalism, infanticide, and a never-ending blood bath of tribal warfare. Four years in, Paton and a friend found themselves surrounded by a mob intent on murder and a meal. In those frightful moments he prayed, remembering who was ultimately in charge of his life:

> I realised that I was immortal till my Master's work with me was done. The assurance came to me, as if a voice out of heaven had spoken, that not a musket would be fired to wound us, not a club prevail to strike us, not a spear leave the hand in which it was held vibrating to be thrown, not an arrow leave the bow, or killing stone the fingers, without the permission of Jesus Christ.[11]

Paton lost all his possessions in that encounter, but walked away with his life. He lived with assurance and he was ready to die with assurance, because he knew that it was God who sovereignly numbered his days (Psalm 139:16). What gave him peace—and will give us peace when we believe it—is not the promise that everything will go our way but the promise that whatever does come our way, God is sovereign over that too. The reality of God's sovereignty is the fear-incinerating, boldness-making, perseverance-producing antidote to everything that would ever trouble us.

A MESSAGE FROM OUR FUTURE SELVES

If we want to live with assurance, we need to look much, much higher than our own grit or ingenuity. We need to look to the same place the rest of heaven has fixed their eyes:

> *After this I looked, and behold, a great multitude that no one could number ... crying out with a loud voice, "Salvation belongs to our God who sits on the throne, and to the Lamb!" (Revelation 7:9-10)*

Don't lose sight of the fact that these words were written to
Christians undergoing immense and systematic persecution at
the end of the first century, under the brutal reign of Emperor
Domitian, who had titled himself *Dominus et Deus*—"Lord
and God." What does the apostle John—writing from exile
himself—give to these Christians to face the troubles of their
day? He gives them a vision of *Christ on the throne*. He gives to
God's people a confidence-inspiring message from their future
selves. And the message of the great redeemed multitude—
coming loud and triumphantly from around the throne—is
sung back into time with zero degrees of doubt: "Salvation
belongs to our God who sits on the throne." This was God's
mission all along. Every one of his promises was fulfilled.
Every one of his purposes was accomplished. And every loss
suffered, prayer uttered, and risk taken by his people was
never in vain.

What will you lean on when dark days come? Or to state
it another way, how big is your view of God? Your theology
around the sovereignty of God is immensely practical. For
there are days in your future that are going to knock you to
the ground. There are situations on your horizon, presently
unknown to you, that will expose just how *not* sovereign *you*
are. Disappointment will make its mark, despair will coil
around your heart, disease will rob your family, death will
strike without warning. Where will you look when the skies
turn black?

Here's where: you look higher.

In the same way the sun shines with uninterrupted
constancy above every clouded sky, so is Christ reigning over
every difficult circumstance. If God is ultimate in authority,
we needn't be held hostage by our anxieties, because our lives
are held securely in the hands of a loving Father, who is also
the King. Peter tells us, "Humble yourselves, therefore, under
the mighty hand of God ... casting all your anxieties on him,

because he cares for you" (1 Peter 5:6-7). He is inviting us to exhale all our fears to the God who cares for us, and who can actually do something about them.

Where in your life do you need to believe *God is sovereign even over this*? Where do you need to breathe in the doctrine of God's sovereignty, so that you may breathe out everything that frightens you?

The risen Jesus is sovereign over everything. You can follow him with total assurance into anything.

REFLECTING AND APPLYING

1. Think about the statement, "Every Christian is a recovering control freak." In what areas is this still true for you?

2. How does a bigger view of God's rule and reign help your mind to rest?

3. What specific fears can you exhale, as you inhale the truth of God's sovereignty?

4. How does understanding that Jesus is sovereign over his mission embolden you to live with daily intentionality on his mission, by sharing the gospel, loving your neighbour, and making disciples?

CHAPTER THREE

God is Unrivalled: The Experience of Embracing Weakness

"God created the world out of nothing, and as long as we are nothing, he can make something out of us."
MARTIN LUTHER

Here's a universal truth: humans don't like feeling helpless. Not one bit. We desire strength. We'll readily take the illusion of having our lives all together, rather than the reality of admitting we are needy, limited, and weak. Power just seems so *right*.

Besides, a smooth, compelling voice seems to tell us, *Wouldn't relying on yourself make you less of an inconvenience to everyone? And to God? Wouldn't that be a better way to live?*

If you've ever felt those words deep within you, then you have heard the whisper of the serpent. The desire to be freed from the limits of creaturely dependence is what broke the world. So we don't need to fear our smallness. In fact, it is only when we acknowledge that God stands alone in unrivalled power that we begin to see the world around us clearly and to live in it rightly. Because if God is all-powerful, we can finally get honest with ourselves and stop pretending that *we* are.

GOD IS UNRIVALLED

When we talk about rivals, we usually imagine two people or teams of equal strength who are battling it out in a reasonably even contest. They're rivals precisely because they're in the same league—either one could win. But to say that God is unrivalled is to confess that he is in his own league. He has all power—he is "omnipotent." While the sovereignty of God speaks to the authority of his reign, the omnipotence of God describes his power to accomplish the purposes of that reign. He has *all* power, which is why over and again he is referred to in Scripture as *Almighty*.

Let's be clear: when it comes to might, God has no rival. Were we to play a game of contrasts, where I asked you to respond with the direct opposite of a word—"boy" (girl), "dog" (cat), "kale" (happiness) and so on—if I were to ask what was the opposite to "God," your instinct might be to respond with "Satan." But you would be wrong. The opposite to Satan—that wicked, fallen angel—would be another angel, another created being.

The opposite to God is *nothing*:

> *To whom will you liken me and make me equal, and compare me, that we may be alike? (Isaiah 46:5)*

God has no equal, which means God has no opposite who can match him, no rival to his might, no competitor for his throne. Satan may well be rebelliously opposed to the purposes of God, but the strength of his evil is limited, while the strength of Almighty God is limitless. Add together all the strength and brilliance and cunning of every person, society, institution, and nation, and it would total no more than a drop in a bucket or a speck of dust on a scale (Isaiah 40:15). Or put more bluntly, "All the nations are as nothing before [the Lord], they are accounted by him as less than nothing and emptiness" (Isaiah 40:17). Isaiah is saying that the full strength of humanity pushing against God is a step backward. A minus factor. The equivalent of battling a lightning storm with a metallic rod or fighting off a tornado with a kite.

Being unlimited in power means that God has never been fatigued by a task, confused by a problem, or worn out by the responsibilities of his sovereignty. When God "gives power to the faint" (Isaiah 40:29), he gives in a way that never makes him poorer and yet still makes the recipient richer. He does not expend energy that needs to be replenished; he is the undiminishing source of energy. It is as simple for him to create a billion galaxies as it is a blade of grass. The prophet elaborates:

> *Have you not known? Have you not heard?*
> *The LORD is the everlasting God,*
>   *the Creator of the ends of the earth.*
> *He does not faint or grow weary;*
>   *his understanding is unsearchable.*
> *He gives power to the faint,*
>   *and to him who has no might he increases strength.*
> *Even youths shall faint and be weary,*
>   *and young men shall fall exhausted;*
> *but they who wait for the LORD shall renew their strength;*
>   *they shall mount up with wings like eagles;*
> *they shall run and not be weary;*
>   *they shall walk and not faint. (Isaiah 40:28-31)*

If God were limited in his power, then we'd have reason to be concerned. What if God comes up against a problem or an enemy that is stronger than he? But God answers us: *Who in all of existence could possibly fit that description?* God's omnipotence is good news for those who love him. We can have confidence that there is no wickedness too great for God's mercy, no obstacle too great for God's wisdom, no heart too hard for God's love to overcome. Nothing is too complicated for him. No situation is beyond him. No one is too far from him. He is able to accomplish exactly what he intends to accomplish. He is *El-Shaddai—the God who is Almighty.*

THE UPWARD REACH OF DEATH

Given the might of God's unrivalled divinity, is it any wonder that Scripture repeatedly warns us that "God opposes the proud" (James 4:6; see also 1 Peter 5:5; Proverbs 16:5; Isaiah 2:12; Jeremiah 50:31; Daniel 4:37)? He opposes that which is deadly to us, and our constant reaching for glory and power is as destructive as it is demonic. Literally. It all began with Lucifer reaching for God's throne, when the brightest angel was turned into the darkest of devils. Adam and Eve followed Satan's glory hunger when they reached for God's knowledge through a forbidden fruit and fractured all of creation. The builders of Babel reached for the heavens and were humbled into the dust. In the book of Esther, Haman reached for position and power, only to find that at the top of the staircase of self-exaltation was not a crown but a noose. The Babylonian King Nebuchadnezzar reached for a glory that God warned him away from in a dream, and traded life in the palace for life in the pasture. No one "falls" into hell. Without Christ, we climb there with one upward reach for stolen glory at a time. C.S. Lewis writes:

> In God you come up against something which is in every respect immeasurably superior to yourself. Unless you know God as that—and, therefore, know yourself as nothing in comparison—you do not know God at all. As long as you are proud you cannot know God. A proud man is always looking down on things and people; and, of course, as long as you are looking down, you cannot see something that is above you.[12]

Have you noticed this about yourself? We look down on others on a nearly daily basis. That's how pride works; it is constantly comparing; constantly seeking a glory that comes from elevating ourselves above another. And Lewis is saying, *That way of living will destroy us.* When we grab for glory, sooner or later we'll inevitably bring back a fist full of misery. But when we embrace our weakness; when we make peace with what we are in light of who *God* is; when we stoop low with John the Baptist, convinced in our hearts that "[Jesus] must increase, but I must decrease" (John 3:30); there in the low place, we become most fully alive and most fully ourselves. For the low place is where the path of Jesus leads us, if we are willing to follow him there.

"God opposes the proud," but as James continues, he "gives grace to the humble" (James 4:6b). In the low place of humility, we actually come alive.

HUMILITY: THE DOWNWARD PATH OF LIFE

What does it mean to truly be humble? Humility is a life lived rightly before God, as we increasingly learn to see the reality that the centre of life is not ourselves but God. So in a very important way, humility does not mean we are self-loathing, but God-focused. It is not self-hatred, but self-forgetfulness.

Think about it: have you ever been around another Christian who isn't preoccupied with proving themselves to you or trying to impress you; a person who just demonstrated a genuine interest in you? That person is living in the freedom that only humility can give. And the absence of posturing and self-promotion is like a breath of mountain air to your soul. Because they are secure in Christ, they're not trying to impress you. And because they've quit trying to impress you, they're free to sincerely love you. You walk away from their presence feeling you've just experienced a measure of Christ himself. Because, you have.

But to aim for humility directly is to miss it entirely—we will only become proud of our pursuit! Instead, the only way to become more humble is to get our eyes off ourselves altogether, and fix them solely upon Jesus. As one author has put it:

> To look at our humility is to make it vanish; to look at the infinitely lovely God, supremely manifest in Christ, is to bring humility in the back door of the heart.[13]

So let's behold him together.

THE LION WHO IS THE LAMB

Jesus is God's perfect picture of strength contained in weakness. In Revelation 5, John paints a breathtaking heavenly portrait of this divine tension. In his vision, John is told by one who is with him, "See, the Lion of the tribe of Judah … has triumphed" (Revelation 5:5, NIV). Yet when he looks, it is not a lion that he sees at all: "Then I saw a Lamb, looking as if it had been slain, standing at the centre of the throne" (v 6). Jesus is both the Lion that has conquered and the Lamb that was slain.

When we think of a lion, we think of nobility. Kingliness. In Jesus we see unmatched power, unrivalled glory, and unparalleled strength. He is the one who moment by moment, "upholds the universe by the word of his power" (Hebrews 1:3). He is the perfect embodiment of both the "power of God and the wisdom of God" (1 Corinthians 1:24). He has a name that is far above every other name, and a power that transcends every other power (Ephesians 1:21).

Yet he was also the Lamb who willingly went to a cross as our sacrifice. And all the while, he was taunted, *If you're really the Messiah, save yourself and call down angels.* And he gave no answer. He breathed his last, and was laid in a tomb. And his disciples despaired. And hell celebrated. And the world hummed quietly along through that holy weekend, as if Jesus' life had been of no consequence at all. When we think of a lamb, we think of weakness.

But on the third day, the "Lamb who was slain" was raised with resurrection power! In Jesus we see victory gained through dying; might displayed through humility. We see this dynamic constantly play out in books and films—as the Dark Lord's kingdom of evil is overthrown through the smallness of a hobbit. We celebrate it in history—as a Black preacher dismantled a government-endorsed system of racism through non-violent resistance. And if these stories thrill our hearts, how much more so the pinnacle of God's power being revealed through the lowliness of a cross? How can this be? Because "the foolishness of God is wiser than men, and the weakness of God is stronger than men" (1 Corinthians 1:25). Jesus' shed blood counterintuitively becomes the grounds for our forgiveness, the means of our conquering, and the boast of our good news (Revelation 12:11).

Kingliness and weakness. Is it any wonder that John records countless myriads and millions of voices saying with a loud voice, "Worthy is the Lamb who was slain, to receive power..." (Revelation 5:12)? Only in Jesus does perfected power and perfected humility dwell together in perfect harmony.

Jesus not only holds the mighty power that we need, he also shows us how the way of weakness is the pathway into that power. Jesus said, "Everyone who exalts himself will be humbled, but the one who humbles himself will be exalted" (Luke 18:14). Why is this biblical principle so frequently repeated across the Old and New Testaments and so vital to a right experience of God? Read that verse again slowly. The first half shows the way of the first Adam that led to death, whereas the second half shows us the way of the second Adam—Christ—that leads to life.

The door of pride looks like a royal promotion, but it leads into a prison cell. The door of humility looks like a restriction, but it opens up into an eternal horizon of freedom.

MAKING OUR HOME IN THE LOW PLACE

Your weakness, then, is not an inconvenience to avoid. On the contrary, it is the blood-stained doorway that your Saviour opened, that leads you into a life marked by the power of the Spirit and the strength of Almighty God. God meets you in the low place. Humility is the holy ground upon which you can encounter the God of power in a way that won't destroy you, but revive you:

> For thus says the One who is high and lifted up, who inhabits eternity, whose name is Holy: "I dwell in the high and holy place, and also with him who is of a contrite and lowly spirit, to revive the spirit of the lowly, and to revive the heart of the contrite." (Isaiah 57:15)

God dwells in the "high and holy place." Notice it is he alone who dwells there, "the One" who is high and lifted up, utterly unrivalled. It is this place that the suicidal tendencies of our sin—our pride—are drawn toward like a moth to a lamp. But there's another place that the God of infinite strength also dwells: "with him who is of a contrite and lowly spirit." And there in the low place, where we embrace our creaturely limitations, God revives us with his power. So we don't need to be afraid of weakness. That's our gospel-superpower.

The final letter that the 18th-century minister John Wesley wrote, six days before his death, was to a young man with the last name of Wilberforce. With the latter facing a humanly impossible, uphill battle of abolishing the evil of slave-trading, the older Wesley wrote:

Unless God has raised you up for this very thing, you
will be worn out by the opposition of men and devils;
but if God be for you, who can be against you? Are all
of them together stronger than God? … Go on, in the
name of God and in the power of his might.[14]

We may not have the same task before us as Wilberforce.
But we do have the same God behind us. So what is it you
feel too worn out to accomplish? Where do the obstacles or
opposition feel simply insurmountable? "Go on, in the name
of God and in the power of his might."

EMBRACING THE WEAKNESS OF PRAYER

The New Testament also speaks to those of us who are prone
to being too sure of ourselves. Perhaps for many of us, the
greatest indicator of pride in our hearts is not the presence of
boasting but the absence of prayer. We often identify pride
through really obvious things like bragging, boasting, and
name-dropping. But if I want to discover the most accurate
measure of self-reliance in my own life, I need look no further
than within the mirror of my prayer-life.

Relying on our own cleverness to live out the Christian life
is like trying to circle the globe in a glider. It might fly for a
while, but predictably, it is going to crash. Prayer, on the other
hand, is God's sovereignly appointed means of connecting our
never-ending neediness to God's never-ending power. Prayer is
the vehicle through which God will accomplish his invincible
purposes, through the lives of weak, dependent people, like
you and me. When our lives are absent of dependent prayer,
they are absent of divine power. What is it—big or small—that
burdens your heart today? Have you prayed about it? Or merely
strategized about it, worried over it, or thrown in the towel on it?

Prayer is not an afterthought for those who can mostly
handle their lives but need a leg-up for the really hard stuff.

Prayer is daily bread for the starving and oxygen for the drowning. And if that's not incentive enough to embrace the weakness of prayer, God reminds us in Romans 8:26-27 that "the Spirit helps us in our weakness." When all human vocabulary runs out, the Spirit's help does not. When our words are reduced to mere groans that escape our lips in a Godward direction, the Spirit himself hears the prayer-within-the-prayer and "intercedes for us ... according to the will of God." No wonder J.I. Packer reminds us, "Don't fret; just pray. God fixes our prayers on the way up! If he does not answer the prayer we made, he will answer the prayer we should have made. That is all anyone needs to know."[15]

CHEERFULLY COMING TO THE END OF OURSELVES
Here we find one of the great paradoxes of the kingdom. We cannot succeed until we come to the place of humility in which we realise: I cannot do this. So why don't we just go ahead and own it? All we have to lose is a high view of ourselves. And that was going to destroy us anyways. Our problem is not our weakness but a self-reliant cleverness, which keeps us from relying upon God. It is our seeming strength—our addiction to our own capability—that closes the door of God's power in our life. This is what the theologian Francis Schaeffer described as the central problem of our age for Christians (including those with good theology): our tendency "to do the Lord's work in the power of the flesh instead of in the power of the Spirit."[16]

We all have two choices: we can pretend to be more impressive than we are. Or we can embrace weakness, make our home in the low place, and cultivate a poverty of spirit that makes space for God the Holy Spirit to renew us again and show off what only he can do. In the place of our confessed weakness, God reveals his unstoppable power. Every trial and pressure and devil that you face are all *smaller* than the God who made you and loves you.

When we become convinced of God's unrivalled power enough to grab hold of our creaturely dependence, and gladly come to the end of ourselves, we too will be able to say, "Therefore I will boast all the more gladly of my weaknesses, so that the power of Christ may rest upon me" (2 Corinthians 12:9b).

Isn't that good news? God doesn't want your strength. Never did. Never will.

He wants to give you his.

REFLECTING AND APPLYING

1. What are some ways you are tempted to go to the "high place" of pride, rather than the "low place" of humility?

2. List one or two specific areas in your life that you have perhaps been trying to make progress in through your own cleverness, and that you sense God wants you to bring to him in prayer?

3. How does understanding that God is all-powerful free us to stop chasing after impressiveness?

CHAPTER FOUR

God is Never Far Away: The Experience of Courage

"The one thing we owe absolutely to God, is never to be afraid of anything."
CHARLES DE FOUCAULD

Driving home with my family one warm summer evening, we rounded the corner and eyed a monstrous-sized python crossing our street barely 100 metres from our house. We live in Australia, so snakes aren't unusual. But this one was on another level—its long, patterned body spanned nearly the entire width of the road. I quickly parked the car, and naturally, all seven of us rushed to get a closer look. My four-year-old twins placed their little hands in mine, drawing courage from my presence. With the sun setting we were losing light, so after observing from a (reasonably) safe distance, we began walking back up the hill to our house. On the way my eldest challenged me to race to the front door. Never one to turn down a competition, I accepted. The trash-talking began. A head-start was granted. And everyone was off, sprinting toward our driveway.

There's something delightfully pathetic about an out-of-shape grown man, furiously pumping his arms and legs past a group of children in a foot-race. But there I was, striding shame-free and triumphant across our driveway, arms raised like I had just dethroned Usain Bolt from his podium.

The sweet sensation of victory, though, was short lived.

A child's terror-filled scream pierced the night.

The kind you hear in horror movies; the kind that sends a parent's heart into their throat. I turned quickly, hurrying toward the sound. It was Elyana, our youngest daughter, flying up the hill as fast as her little four-year-old legs would carry her, tears streaming down her face, eyes wide with panic. Scooping her into my arms, between great heaving sobs, I pieced the story together.

She didn't realise there was a race.

Lost in her thoughts on the short walk home, she looked up to see all her older siblings running away, as fast as they possibly could. Followed by her Dad sprinting away, as fast as he possibly could. And of course, her four-year old mind naturally concluded, "THE GIANT SNAKE IS COMING!"

In a split second, it dawned on her: she was in last place.

No wonder she screamed with fear.

As I held her tight, a liquidy substance began to form in my own eyes. I felt like my heart had been ripped right out of me as it dawned on me what must have been going through her mind. In a precious and tender moment together I attempted to explain: *No sweetie, I would never abandon you. If there's danger, your daddy will stand between you and the danger, not run away from it. You never have to be afraid when you're with me.* Her tears eventually settled. And in the arms of her father, so too did her fears.

As many of us have discovered, everything changes when we're in the presence of someone stronger than us, who loves us.

GOD ALWAYS NEAR

Among the many phrases that the great 20th-century theologian Francis Schaeffer contributed to the world was the language of "the God who is there." No matter where *there* is, God is. Because God is not confined to a body *and* because he alone is infinite, there is no space in existence that he is not. He is omnipresent, or all-present—everywhere-present. There is not a molecule of the physical or spiritual universe that is off limits to his "there-ness." David had a sense of God's infinite everywhere-ness when he penned parts of Psalm 139:

> *Where shall I go from your Spirit?*
>   *Or where shall I flee from your presence?*
> *If I ascend to heaven, you are there!*
>   *If I make my bed in Sheol, you are there!*
> *If I take the wings of the morning*
>   *and dwell in the uttermost parts of the sea,*
> *even there your hand shall lead me,*
>   *and your right hand shall hold me.*
> *If I say, "Surely the darkness shall cover me,*
>   *and the light about me be night,"*
> *even the darkness is not dark to you;*
>   *the night is bright as the day,*
>   *for darkness is as light with you. (Psalm 139:7-12)*

The British preacher Charles Spurgeon told the story of an atheist who wrote on a piece of paper, "God is nowhere," then instructed his child to read it. The child read it aloud as "God is now-here." It was the truth instead of a lie, and it pierced the man's own heart, eventually leading him to Christ. To the rebellious heart, God's omnipresence described in Psalm 139 is understandably unnerving—God is everywhere and sees everything. Nothing escapes his gaze. But to those who love him and long for him—who cry out with the psalmist, "For me it is good to be near God" (Psalm 73:28)—his omnipresence soothes us with both comfort and courage. For if God is everywhere, then God is always near.

But we can go even deeper. Not only is God boundlessly present in *where* he is, he has no limits of *when* he is; he simultaneously inhabits every place in the universe and every

place in what we call "time." He is "the Alpha and the Omega
… who is and who was and who is to come, the Almighty"
(Revelation 1:8). All of him is in every *where*, and in every
when—past, present, and future.

This all-pervading sense of God's nearness is known as his
immanence. God is, as Tozer describes, "near to everything,
next to everyone, and through Jesus Christ immediately
accessible to every loving heart."[17] Regardless of how we feel
in any given moment, God is "not far from each one of us"
(Acts 17:27).

JESUS: GOD WITH US

In Christ, God came *to* us. Think about that. While we
may celebrate the incarnation of Jesus every December, its
explosive implications for our lives can be so easily missed
among all the planning, parties and presents.

In the incarnation, the Creator who fills all things, embraced
the limitations of a body.

The Almighty swaddled himself with vulnerability.

The Infinite clothed himself with finitude.

The Author put himself on the page.

Comparing every preceding event in history to what took
place that first Christmas would be like holding up a $10
flashlight next to the blinding brilliance of the sun. Salvation
came to us, in an infant who was older than his parents,
along with the created universe. In Christ, the immortal
God who dwells in unapproachable light (1 Timothy 6:16),
made himself visible and approachable. Jesus traded the
glory of heaven for the musty smell of a Bethlehem barn, all
to communicate the message that God had been telling his
covenant people on repeat throughout the Old Testament:
I am with you.

The incarnation reveals that God is not aloof. His
promises are true. He is near, and he wants us to know it; to

bank our very lives on it. It is the truth that we most need to know, that we most often forget, and that emboldens us to face anything.

In fact, God wants to make this so plain to us that he starts and ends the very first book of the New Testament with these same words. In Matthew 1, Jesus comes to us as "'Immanuel' (which means, *God with us*)" (Matthew 1:23). In Matthew 28, moments before he ascends into heaven, the risen Jesus commissions his followers to "Go ... and make disciples of all nations," on a mission that would cost nearly all of them their lives. But he follows it up with the promise, "Behold, *I am with you always*, to the end of the age" (Matthew 28:19-20), declaring even on his departure, that he is not going anywhere. He will continue to be near. He is still Immanuel—God with us—the one who knows our human experience from the inside out.

But it gets even better than that...

THE HOLY SPIRIT: GOD WITHIN US

For the Christian, not only is God near us through his omnipresence, and with us through the person and work and promises of Jesus, but he also takes up residence *within* us through the indwelling of the Holy Spirit. The Christian not only has God around them and God with them, but God *within* them! Paul reminded the Christians in Corinth, "Do you not know that *you* are God's temple and that God's Spirit dwells in you?" (1 Corinthians 3:16).

Here lies the difference between a general sense of God's proximity and a special sense of his intimacy through the Holy Spirit. This explains the ways in which Scripture describes God as being "far from the wicked" (Proverbs 15:29) and Christians as those who "once were far off," but who have now "been brought near by the blood of Christ" (Ephesians 2:13). Being far from God isn't about spatial distance, but relational distance due to sin. Therefore, as Sam Storms points out, "Drawing 'near' to God does not require a journey, only repentance, faith, and humility."[18]

What a wonderful, courage-producing truth: living inside of every flawed, imperfect child of God is the same power which formed the universe and clothed the Crucified One with resurrection glory. Just take a look at how generously committed the Spirit is to us by reading slowly through the majestic eighth chapter of Romans. The indwelling of the Holy Spirit is God's perpetual reminder to his people that he frees us (Romans 8:2); makes his home within us (v 9); leads us (v 14); assures us (v 16); helps us and intercedes for us (v 26); and that he is for us (v 31). That's why Paul can end the chapter with a stirring declaration that whatever trouble or hardship we face, Christ's people will emerge victorious when all the dust has cleared:

> For I am sure that neither death nor life, nor angels nor rulers, nor things present nor things to come, nor powers, nor height nor depth, nor anything else in all creation, will be able to separate us from the love of God in Christ Jesus our Lord. (Romans 8:38-39)

THE CHRISTIAN LIFE ON TWO LEVELS

Three words from the end of Romans 8 point us toward a fourth layer of God's nearness, that will propel us into our world with unparalleled confidence: "in Christ Jesus."

Not only is God all around us…

Not only is Christ with us…

Not only is the Spirit within us…

Now, because of the work of Jesus on the cross, we are forever "in Christ Jesus."

The New Testament refers to being a "Christian" just three times, but to us being "in Christ" 216 times. So the primary way in which God wants us to understand ourselves is in regards to our unchanging location in proximity to him.

I've heard it illustrated like this. Right now, I'm *in* a building. Likely, so are you. And that reality is going to change multiple times over the coming days and years as we go in and out of different buildings. On one level, our location (in regard to buildings) is constantly changing. But on another level, you and I are both *in* the Solar System. And that is a reality that will never change in our lifetime. In the same way, Christians are always living on two levels; we live in our ever-changing circumstances, but more profoundly, in our never-changing location of "in Christ Jesus." You may have believed in a general sense that "God is everywhere" or even "God is near," but have you ever stopped to consider what being "in Christ Jesus" *actually* means for you?

Beloved Christian: God intends for the constancy of your eternal location to shape the way you navigate your fluctuating circumstances. When dark days turn up to haunt your mind, you face them *in Christ Jesus*. When sickness knocks on your door, you face it *in Christ Jesus*. And when you are confronted by the major and minor troubles of this coming month, you face them *in Christ Jesus*. Yes, you may find yourself in the midst of afflictions or dangers or even the darkness of despair, but more profoundly, *you are in Christ*.

A SWIG OF IRISH COURAGE (NOT THE KIND YOU THINK)

It was this vision of God's immanent presence that powered much of the early Celtic awakening in the fifth century, under a man named Patrick. Abducted as a teenager from his English home by pirates, he spent six years living as a slave amongst the Irish. During this time, the Christian faith of his parents became his own, and one night he attempted a daring escape, successfully making it back across the Irish Sea to England, where he spent the next few decades studying Scripture and building up the church. At around the age of 40, God spoke to him in a dream, commanding him to go back to Ireland to preach the gospel and plant churches, as a missionary to what was then reputed as a violent, drunken, illiterate people whom many had given up all hope of reaching. Patrick obeyed, and spent the rest of his life courageously serving those who had once enslaved him. When he died at the age of 77, he had helped plant over 300 churches and had seen over 100,000 Irish men and women turn to Christ and be baptised. During his difficult years of ministry, he wrote, "Daily, I expect to be murdered or betrayed or reduced to slavery if the occasion arises, but I fear nothing, because of the promises of heaven."

What fuelled such fearlessness in the face of such danger? Patrick was convinced of the nearness of God. He knew *who* was with him. In his most well-known prayer, called "The Breastplate of Saint Patrick," we get a glimpse of the Christ-lens through which he viewed the many troubles and terrors around him:

> Christ be with me, Christ within me,
> Christ behind me, Christ before me,
> Christ beside me, Christ to win me,
> Christ to comfort and restore me.
> Christ beneath me, Christ above me,
> Christ in quiet, Christ in danger,
> Christ in hearts of all that love me,
> Christ in mouth of friend and stranger.

Patrick was convinced that no matter where he was or what he was facing, Christ was with him.

THE ANTIDOTE TO ALL FEAR

Years ago, I was in Ethiopia with a team of pastors to encourage and learn from around 2,000 pastors, evangelists, and leaders from the largest evangelical denomination in the country. In the first few rows sat dozens of older pastors who had spent time in prison for their faithfulness to Christ during the years that Ethiopia was under the heavy hand of communism. Behind them were younger church planters, many of whom faced ongoing persecution as they advanced the gospel into spiritually and physically hostile areas. I had never been in a room so collectively committed to the mission of Jesus, even in the face of very real danger. When it was my turn to preach, I couldn't help ask myself: What in the world could I possibly teach *them*? What words could I say to put fuel in their tanks and give them the resources to face the difficulties that lay outside those walls? Where can any of us look when our present moment calls for courage?

Here's what we need to remember: the experience of courage has much more to do with our eyes than our wills. There's a reason we use the expression "Take courage!" rather than "Make courage!" Courage is not something *generated*, it is *received*. It comes from being in the presence of someone stronger than us, who is for us. That's why when children get scared at night, a good father doesn't yell, "Knock it off, just be brave!" Instead they walk into the room and remind them, "You don't need to be afraid. I'm right here." Have you noticed in Scripture, that this is exactly what God does when his people are afraid?

See if you can spot a recurring theme. When the Israelites were standing on the edge of the promised land, with their enemies ahead of them, God said: "Do not be frightened, and do not be dismayed, for the LORD your God is with you wherever you go" (Joshua 1:9). When, generations later, they were facing exile, God said: "Fear not, for I am with you" (Isaiah 41:9; 43:2-5). When Jeremiah doubted whether he could fulfil God's purposes as a mere youth, God said, "Do not be afraid of them, for I am with you" (Jeremiah 1:7-9). When Jesus sent out his followers to make disciples and proclaim good news to the entire world, he girded his

ADAM RAMSEY

instruction with the promise, "Behold, I am with you always, to the end of age" (Matthew 28:20). When the apostle Paul faced threats and persecution, God said: "Do not be afraid, but go on speaking and do not be silent, for I am with you" (Acts 18:9-10). And whatever you face right now—whatever it is that makes your chest tighten or your mind race or your heart anxious—God says to you what he has said to his people throughout time: *I am with you.*

YOU CAN FACE ANYTHING

In a sin-fractured world marked by instability, God's people need the kind of courage that flows from a certainty of God's nearness. And yet every single one of us will face circumstances in our lives that give us a kind of cosmic separation anxiety.

Maybe this storm will be the one that sinks me...?

Maybe this sin will be the one that Jesus throws in the towel on me...?

Maybe this trial will be the one that I just can't endure...?

Maybe this is the moment I am left to face life alone...?

Time and time again, the antidote to fear and the birthplace of courage, is found in God's promise: "I am with you." The words of Jesus to every struggling, stumbling child of God, is "I will never leave you or abandon you" (Hebrews 13:5 CSB). When we really believe that God is eternally near, our hope is encouraged, our faith is emboldened, our eyes are refocused, our resolve is renewed, and our hands are strengthened. In fact, this is the real secret weapon of Christianity, that sustains us in the darkest moments of the human experience. David reminds us in Psalm 23:4:

> *Even though I walk through the valley of the shadow of death,*
> *I will fear no evil,*
> *for you are with me.*

If God is with us, we have nothing to fear. Not even death. How would your life change, right now, if you knew for certain that moment-by-moment, God himself was with you, sustaining you, never abandoning you, regardless of whether you sensed his nearness or not? You'd never be afraid again.

As I prepared to speak to these Ethiopian church leaders, I realised that in that meeting, my job was not that of instruction but that of reminder. So I told them once again about God's promise of his presence. I reminded them that the same Spirit that raised Christ from the dead was alive in them. I rehearsed the truth that so many already knew, but so greatly needed to hear: *Take courage! The risen Jesus is with you!* For many of us, this doctrine will cause our hearts to leap. For these men and women, it caused their mouths to roar. Seldom have I as a preacher heard such a sound of courage and praise sweep across a room. It still gives me goose-bumps to think of it.

Everything changes when we remember that God is not far. If the gospel is true, if Christ is risen, if the Spirit that raised him from the grave is really within you, if the unrivalled King of glory has promised that he will be with you until the end of the age, then your resources outnumber your difficulties by infinitude. In Christ, you are loaded. You can say with the poet of Psalm 118:6, "The LORD is on my side; I will not fear. What can man do to me?" So take heart! You have more spiritual power available to you than you have spiritual enemies coming at you—no matter how dark your present moment.

REFLECTING AND APPLYING

1. How is God's ever-present "there-ness" a comfort to you?
2. Which of the four ways that God is near to us (God all around us; Jesus with us; the Holy Spirit within us; we are in Christ) do you most need to remember and why?
3. Think of what makes you afraid. What happens to those fears when you look at them in light of God's promise that he is with you?
4. How would you finish the following sentence? *When I am convinced that God is never far away from me, I...*

CHAPTER FIVE

God is All-holy and All-knowing: The Experience of Honesty

"The temptation to look good without being good is the temptation of the age."
BRENNAN MANNING

The French atheist and philosopher Jean-Paul Sartre tells the story of a man who is enjoying time alone on a park bench when he suddenly becomes aware of the presence of another person in the distance, staring at him. The man is startled out of his serenity into a profoundly uncomfortable awareness of himself. *What does this stranger think of me? Are they judging me? Do they value me? Are they for me or against me?*

We all know what that's like, to feel the stare of another's eyes on us. When he was aware of only himself, the man felt no moral or relational obligations. But the penetrating watchfulness of another person disrupted his sense of autonomy. In Sartre's tale, the man finally discovers that the "other" is merely a mannequin, and he returns to how he was, relieved that it was all just in his mind. He can return to pretending that he answers only to himself.[19]

It's one thing to be under the unsettling gaze of another person, wondering what they think of us. But it's quite another to be under the gaze of a morally perfect, all-knowing God who knows everything about us. Yet God doesn't want us to run from him in terror. He wants us to turn around and stop running. He wants us to be honest.

THE GOD WHO IS HOLY

Both the holiness of God and the omniscience of God have to do with the category of *truth*. The first has to do with embodiment of *moral* truth, the second with the comprehension of *all* truth.

To say that God is holy is to confess that God creates the standard we know as "perfection," and then acts with absolute consistency to that standard, because he alone is that standard. As the psalmist writes in Psalm 145:17, "The LORD is righteous in all his ways, and holy in all his works" (KJV). No other attribute is more used of God in the Scriptures, than that of his holiness. The Greek word for "holy," used 235 times in the New Testament, means "unlike everything else, set apart."

The holy God calls his people to join him in this attribute by pursuing holy lives—lives that are set apart. After delivering the Israelites from Egyptian oppression, God says to his people, "I am the LORD who brought you up out of the land of Egypt to be your God. You shall therefore be holy, for I am holy" (Leviticus 11:45). In case we were tempted to dismiss the Old Testament, Jesus also commands, "You therefore must be perfect, as your heavenly Father is perfect" (Matthew 5:48), and then just for good measure, Peter reminds us, "As he who called you is holy, you also be holy in all your conduct, since it is written, 'You shall be holy, for I am holy'" (1 Peter 1:15-16). The pattern of Scripture seems pretty clear. While nobody is saved *through* their own holiness of life, those who are saved have been called *to* a holiness of life, because such a life reflects the God who delivered them—the God who is holy.

THE GOD WHO KNOWS ALL

If God's holiness sets him apart in his moral perfection, his omniscience reminds us that he is perfect in knowledge and understanding. To say that he is the *God who knows*, is to say in the same breath that he is the *God who does not learn*. How can he? He knows every detail of what was, what is, and what will be. Not only that, he is intimately acquainted with every possibility that *could* be, but won't be. Nothing is mystery to him, nothing is concealed from him; before him all of existence stands exposed for what it is, as it *truly* is. God is "perfect in knowledge" (Job 37:16).

From the immense knowledge of how many stars and planets adorn his universe, to the intimate awareness of every thought that has ever passed through your mind, to the relationship between every single action along with their corresponding reactions—all that blends together to create the mega-symphony of matter, sound, energy, beauty, and beings that we label "existence"—and God knows it all. Cosmic and microscopic. Past and future. At every level, with complete precision, without strain, and without coffee. No wonder Paul cries out, "Oh, the depth of the riches and wisdom and knowledge of God!" (Romans 11:33).

THE GOD WHO KNOWS US

It goes without saying then, that if God knows every part of existence, then he knows every part of us. There is not one molecule of our lives — in thought, motive, word, or action—that he is not intimately familiar with. All is laid bare before him. "The LORD searches all hearts and understands every plan and thought" (1 Chronicles 28:9). David writes of God's limitless insight into each of us:

> O LORD, *you have searched me and known me!*
> *You know when I sit down and when I rise up;*

you discern my thoughts from afar.
You search out my path and my lying down
and are acquainted with all my ways.
Even before a word is on my tongue,
behold, O LORD, you know it altogether.

(Psalm 139:1-4)

Our coming and going, our thinking and speaking, the Lord knows us entirely. Quite understandably then, in light of God's holiness and our own falling short of the divine standard, God's unfiltered knowledge of us can be unsettling. He knows all of our jealous thoughts; he sees all lustful fantasies; he hears all our gossip and grumbling. Like Adam and Eve hiding from the Lord in the garden, we too feel the shame of our own moral nakedness, as we consider ourselves in God's light. We feel the weight of Hebrews 4:13 reminding us that "no creature is hidden from his sight, but all are naked and exposed to the eyes of him to whom we must give account." Where will we turn after such a verse? Where does God want us to go with that truth?

Well, we just go to the next verse:

Since then we have a great high priest who has passed
through the heavens, Jesus, the Son of God, let us hold fast
our confession. For we do not have a high priest who is
unable to sympathize with our weaknesses, but one who in
every respect has been tempted as we are, yet without sin.

(Hebrews 4:14-15)

Throughout the book of Hebrews, Jesus is identified as our high priest. In the Old Testament, the role of the high priest was to represent God's people to God, to make atonement for their sins by offering gifts and sacrifices, and to intercede on their behalf. In these same roles—representation, atonement, and intercession—Jesus our great high priest gives us three wonderful gospel-gifts that transform the experience of being under God's eye from the scolding look of a judge to the tender gaze of a Father.

THE GIFT OF CHRIST'S PERFECT OBEDIENCE

Jesus is the Son of God, fully human and fully divine, who walked for 33 years in this world "yet without sin" (Hebrews 4:15). Jesus is both fully God and fully man; the first qualifies him to be our redeemer, and the second qualifies him to be our representative. Both are essential for Jesus to be our "great high priest" who is not aloof from us or unaware of the testings we face in this world. He experienced them all and then some. What a gloriously comforting thought! The all-holy, all-knowing God of glory sympathises with our struggle against temptation. But unlike us, Jesus aced every test. He flawlessly obeyed the Father at every turn.

Here is where this becomes good news for struggling saints: on the cross, in what has been called "the great exchange," Jesus not only—as we're about to see—took our sin and its punishment onto himself, he also clothed us with his own righteousness. Theologians describe this as "gift-righteousness." It's the undeserved gift of Christ's own perfect moral track record.

So beloved Christian, have you failed this past week? Let me rephrase: were you alive this past week? Jesus is your perfect and holy representative. When God looks upon his struggling saints, he sees us on the basis of Christ's perfect work for us, not our imperfect week we tried to live for him.

THE GIFT OF CHRIST'S BLOOD

Not only did Jesus the Holy One live for us; he died for us. The following chapters of Hebrews capture the once-and-for-all-ness of this gift of Christ's blood: "For by one sacrifice he has made perfect forever those who are being made holy"

(Hebrews 10:14, NIV). Did you catch that? The perfection God demands, Christ supplies; even as we struggle onward in this lifelong process of "being made holy." To borrow the language of Romans, we have "been justified by his blood" (Romans 5:9).

Justification is a courtroom word that means the charges have been dropped, innocence has been declared, and the case is closed. To be justified is to receive by faith the verdict that Paul gives in Romans 8:1: "There is therefore now no condemnation for those who are in Christ Jesus." That tiny little two-letter word "no" is loaded with honesty-creating impact. When I wonder in light of my latest sin if God is finally done with me, "no" shouts to my heart, "Not now and not ever!"

I was recently talking with one of my kids as I tucked them into bed. They'd had a rough day of not listening to their mother, facing the consequences, and battling with condemnation from their own heart. They looked up at me through eyes filled with despair and desperation, and in a moment of searching honesty confessed, "Dad, sometimes I'm not sure I'm even a Christian." I asked why they thought that. They answered, "Because I just kept on doing bad things today."

Hasn't every one of us, if we're being honest, had days like that? Years like that? Romans 8:33-34 brings the reinforcements our hearts need to hear in moments like these:

> *Who shall bring any charge against God's elect? It is God who justifies. Who is to condemn? Christ Jesus is the one who died—more than that, who was raised—who is at the right hand of God, who indeed is interceding for us.*

Like Sartre's man on a park bench, we're haunted by condemnation. The expectations of our boss or family members can condemn our best efforts. The behaviour of our children may condemn our parenting. The dark thoughts in our hearts, the ruthless self-talk in our minds, the digits on our bank statement or bathroom scales can all speak a word of condemnation over us. In response to all of these and more, Paul asks, "Who is to condemn?" He's asking, *Who will overrule God's verdict in a believer's life?* The answer is, *No one*. Not Satan. Not others. Not even our own hearts. For the believer, every accusation—regardless of its origin—now contains as much condemning power as a nerf gun has killing power. God's verdict is the final word about our standing with him. J.D. Greear wonderfully sums this up, writing, "Christ's obedience is so spectacular there is nothing we could do to add to it; his death so final that nothing could take away from it."[20]

THE GIFT OF CHRIST'S VOICE

Jesus the great high priest is also our intercessor. To intercede means to stand in the gap on behalf of another. Look again at the present work of Jesus on behalf of his people in Romans 8:34: "Christ Jesus ... is at the right hand of God ... interceding for us." Jesus—the Holy One who knows everything about me— lived out the obedience I couldn't, died condemned where I should've, and now commits to raising his voice with constancy on my behalf. That is how committed he is to finishing the work he has begun in you.

Where justification is Christ's once-and-for-all work for us on the cross, intercession speaks to Christ's ongoing work for us from his throne. Every time you sin, Jesus is standing in heaven like your defence attorney, pointing to his wounds on your behalf. As Hebrews 7:25 declares: "He is able to save to the uttermost those who draw near to God through him, since he always lives to make intercession for them."

Jesus' continued intercession for us means, in the words of the author Dane Ortlund:

Those crevices of sin are themselves the places where Christ loves us the most. His heart willingly goes there. His heart is most strongly drawn there. He knows us to the uttermost, and he saves us to the uttermost, because his heart is drawn out to us to the uttermost.[21]

Christian, Jesus is not fed up with you. And there is never coming a day in your future where he will throw in the towel on you. He saves "to the uttermost." The God who knows it all, the God who made it all, the God above it all, deals tenderly with sinners who come to him with honesty about their need. So why keep hiding? Instead, he invites you to come to him readily and continually with honest confession and repentance. He wants you to come home.

CONQUERING THROUGH CONFESSION

All sin has its power in deception. It is a monster disguised as a supermodel, a beast pretending to be a beauty, a predator posing as a friend. And the power of any specific sin in our lives will be no greater than the degree to which we allow it to live and grow in the darkness. Sin festers in the dark, and is incinerated in the light:

> *If we walk in the light, as he is in the light, we have fellowship with one another, and the blood of Jesus his Son cleanses us from all sin. If we say we have no sin, we deceive ourselves, and the truth is not in us. If we confess our sins, he is faithful and just to forgive us our sins and to cleanse us from all unrighteousness. (1 John 1:7-9)*

John is not saying that through confession of sin we are re-justified over and over, as if every time we sin God changes his verdict about our salvation. Instead, John is calling Christians to an honesty of life that doesn't pretend "we have no sin," but at the same time seeks to make war on sin by exposing it constantly to the light. He is saying that through confession, our legal status in heaven of being righteous in Christ becomes tangible as we *experience* the cleansing power of the blood of Christ. All he requires from us is the courage of honesty. Ray Ortlund has said, "We don't conquer our sins by heroic willpower, we just confess them to death!"[22] Why hold back? Why not go all in with real Christianity—Christianity in the light—where you will be able to win *more* of those battles with specific sins in your life?

We may be able to con those around us into thinking we're pretty godly, but none of us can outsmart God. How could we? His knowledge of us is total, which means he has infinitely more strategies for bringing us into the freedom of honesty than we have for dodging him. Our good Father "disciplines the one he loves … for our good, that we may share his holiness" (Hebrews 12:6, 10). He is more for us than we could ever imagine; his discipline is mercy, not punishment. So why not trust him? All we have to lose is the exhaustion of living a double-life.

And as those verses in 1 John indicate, walking in the light is something we do in "fellowship with one another" (1 John 1:7). Talking with an older mentor over dinner one evening, I remember him looking me square in the eye and asking, "Adam, who knows you and loves you, and isn't the slightest bit impressed by you?" That was one of the most important questions anybody has ever asked me. There are few things more important to our sanctification and sanity than a friend or two among whom there are no secrets. Friendships marked by vulnerability, grace, and truth. Do you have any friendships like this? If you don't, cultivate them. And here's how to start: be honest. Talk about your struggles and failures. And as you do, you'll discover how honest confession leads you into the freedom of repentance along with a gradually increasing holiness of life.

GOD IS NOT DISILLUSIONED WITH YOU

The gospel means that I'm not all that awesome. But I am loved. And that's awesome. The gospel frees me to be honest about the ways I fall short instead of being crushed by them, because it reminds me that Jesus was crushed for me. The gospel means I don't have to hide, because the good news of what the holy and all-knowing Saviour did on the cross is true for me too. The gospel means I don't need to impress, because Christ has eternally secured for me the smile of my Maker. If that's true, then let's burn those useless fig leaves of our self-justifying excuses and lean wholly into the justification of God. As my friend Alex Early has written, "Jesus is not in love with some future version of you or what you used to be. He loves you right where you are, sitting in that chair."[23]

Do you hate your sin? Do you find yourself turning to Jesus again and again with cries of confession and desires for change? Then take heart, beloved struggler. You are undoubtedly a child of God. The fact that you *are* fighting sin is the evidence of spiritual *life*. Dead things don't fight, only living things do. So press onward into the light of holiness.

God will not despise our honesty; he meets us in it with renewing tenderness; he rushes to us there and smothers our confessions with kisses of acceptance. We often think that honesty makes us poorer. But judging from the Father's reaction to his prodigal son's return, we could not be more wrong. He dignifies our repentance with the family ring, reminding us of our true identity. Honesty means exchanging the pig food of our sins for the banquet of God's grace; the tattered clothes of our foolish decisions for the clean suit of Christ's sinlessness; the cold loneliness of the mud, for the warm embrace of the Father. It is the way back home.

How would your own pursuit of holiness change, how might you honestly embrace life in the light, if you became convinced that the doorway of openness before God and others does not lead *into* a prison but *out* of one? Here is the power to stop pretending. Jesus is not disillusioned with you, because he never had any illusions about who you ever were in the first place. He knew exactly, precisely, completely who you are and gave his life for you. Not the Instagrammable you; the *real* you. He knows *that* you to the depths of your being and commits to loving, disciplining, and sanctifying all the way to glory. It is here, and only here, in the place of honesty, that our hearts can find shelter from every condemning accusation, even as we press onward into the beauty of holiness.

REFLECTING AND APPLYING

1. If God is perfect in both his holiness and knowledge of all things, why do you think we still try and hide from him and one another?

2. We all need a couple of people in our life that "know us, love us, and aren't the slightest bit impressed with us. Who might fit this category for you?

3. Read Hebrews 7:25 again. How does knowing that Jesus is interceding for you in your failures change the way you deal with those failures?

4. What are one or two areas of your life that you've been trying to conquer through heroic willpower, which God wants you to start confessing to death by bringing them into the light?

CHAPTER SIX

God is Good: The Experience of Trusting through Suffering

"Taste and see that the LORD is good. How happy is the person who takes refuge in him!"
PSALM 34:8, CSB

There was once a man with a three-letter name from a two-letter town called Job of Uz. And as the story goes, Job was a godly man who loved good, hated evil, and whose life was blessed with thousands of tangible evidences of God's goodness toward him (Job 1:1-5).

Then one day, in what is undoubtedly one of the most confusing and bizarre encounters recorded in Scripture, Satan comes before God and challenges him that the only reason Job reveres God is because God has so generously blessed his life. *Remove his blessings,* taunts Satan, *and he will surely curse you to your face* (v 6-11). And remarkably, God allows it. Within a single day, Satan robs Job of everything dear in his life. His children, servants, possessions, and wealth—gone. Yet through the tears of his grief Job responds, "The LORD gave, and the LORD has taken away; blessed be the name of the LORD" (v 20). A second time, Satan rages upon righteous Job, afflicting him "with loathsome sores from the sole of his foot to the crown of his head" (2:7), sparing only his life, a nagging wife who counsels him to "curse God and die," and a few awful friends who try to convince Job that God must be angry with him. Yet from the bottom of the valley of pain in the midst of his laments, Job declares, "Though He slay me, yet will I trust Him" (3:15, NKJV).

A GROANING WORLD

The book of Job is a biblical manifesto on suffering. Job instructs us with the same lesson that the pirate Westley offers the princess in the classic movie, *The Princess Bride*: "Life is pain, highness. Anyone who says different is selling something." For all of us in varying degrees, suffering has scraped us and shaped us. In Romans 8:18-23, the apostle Paul describes this present age awaiting the return of Jesus as one of groaning. Not only we ourselves but "the whole creation" groans like a woman in labour, awaiting the coming of new life (v 22-23). But whether it is the groan of our own sin or another's sin against us; whether it's the pain of unfulfilled hopes, unmet expectations, unexpected sickness, or undeniable spiritual warfare, we all soon discover that pain is a normal part of the human experience.

A younger version of me thought that I might be the exception. But the first five years of planting a church quickly rid me of that delusion. Reflecting back one evening with my wife, Kristina, we realised that our combined experiences during this period included:

- being publicly and privately slandered
- being betrayed and lied to,
- being cussed out,
- being physically threatened,
- being depressed,
- being completely broke, with bank accounts in the negative,
- being held at gunpoint (Adam, not Kristina),

- being pregnant with twins (Kristina, not Adam),
- being poisoned by a doctor, leading to ten Emergency Room trips over a two-month period (also Kristina),
- someone trying to hijack the direction of our young church,
- someone trying to break into our home,
- losing family members to cancer,
- losing friends,
- losing staff,
- and losing our five-year-old in the Australian bush, as the sun was going down, with police search units and rescue dogs being sent to help find him (thankfully, we found him).

But we're not complaining; we know that many have experienced far worse. While our first five years of church planting had its difficulties, it didn't leave us empty-handed. We also gained some wisdom, memories, and friends (along with a few extra grey hairs and kilograms) and experienced much joy along the way. We learned first-hand that we inhabit a world fractured by sin yet soaked in common grace. There will be highs and lows. Laughing and weeping. Glories and groans. This *is* life. The human experience is beautiful, but in a way that is going to kill every one of us.

LEARNING TO TRUST WITH A BLOODY NOSE
Go ahead and look back upon your own life. Do you see the same combination of glories and groans? Most of us come hurtling out of our school years with a vision of how life is supposed to go. But then, over time, *real life* happens. And real life is hard. We enter into the pain of short phrases that pack knockout punches, like, *We're over... I hate you... You're fired... It's cancer... They're gone.* No matter how nimble you are, one day the circumstances of your life back you into a corner and throw a right hook that you aren't able to duck.

Like Eve walking outside to the body of a murdered son and the absence of another…

Like Abraham hiking a hill with a knife, some wood, and the heir of God's promise…

Like David in the aftermath of his night with Bathsheba…

Like Peter locking eyes with his Lord, whom he had just denied for a third time…

Like Mary staring numbly into space one lonely, confusing, Saturday…

Where do we turn when life implodes, when death visits our family, when cancer knocks on our door, when betrayal shows up unannounced, when depression haunts us like a ghost, when pain becomes to us as a shadow?

From our earliest years, we begin a process of learning how to avoid pain. But what we need most deeply is to learn how to feel pain and then what to do with it. It is here that the Scriptures dignify our sufferings with real honesty, help, and hope. While God may never give us a *why* in this lifetime that explains our pain, he does give us a *who*—the Crucified and Risen One, who entered into it, experienced the worst of it, put a deadline on it, and promised that he would not waste one drop of it. The triune God does not stand aloof from sinners and sufferers; he draws near to us simultaneously as the Father who adopts us, the Saviour who sympathises with us, and the Comforter who helps us. Thus "when we cannot trace God's hand," as the popular paraphrase of Spurgeon goes, "we must learn to trust God's heart."

For what abounds and overflows from the heart of God is steadfast, undiluted goodness.

GOD IS GOOD AND DOES GOOD

God is good, all the time. And all the time, God is good. So goes the well-known call and response of the African-American church, pressing this enduring truth of God's goodness into our hearts. It is this quality of God that calls forth our trust. After all, a divine being like the one we have described in the previous five chapters—completely transcendent; unrivalled in his sovereignty and power and righteousness and knowledge; occupying every square inch of the universe—would be a terrifying God, if he were not also perfect in his goodness. As author Jen Wilkin describes it, "God's goodness is a light that radiates through all his other attributes,"[24] so that his characteristics might draw us near rather than repel us away. A God unrivalled in power who was not also unwavering in goodness might be revered, but certainly could not be trusted.

Yet God is good—*all the time*—which is the reason so frequently given in the psalms for our praise of him and thanks to him (Psalm 100:5; 106:1; 107:1; 118:1, 29; 135:3; 136:1). He is good and does good (Psalm 119:68), and apart from him there is no thing that is "good" (Psalm 16:2).

Not only that, it is his goodness that is the very epicentre of his glory. When Moses meets with God on the mountain in Exodus 33:18 and asks, "Please show me your glory," how did God answer?

> *I will make all my **goodness** pass before you and will proclaim before you my name "The LORD" ... Behold, there is a place by me where you shall stand on the rock, and while my **glory** passes by I will put you in a cleft of the rock, and I will cover you with my hand until I have passed by. (Exodus 33:19-22)*

To behold the goodness of God (v 19) and the glory of God (v 22) is to witness the same thing. The two cannot be separated. His goodness is his glory, and his glory is his goodness.

GOD'S GOODNESS IN THIS WORLD

Goodness flows out of God as naturally as breath flows out of us. When he speaks, a creation that is "good" is what results (see Genesis 1). The morning sun rises, bursting the night's darkness with colour and light and the goodness of God. The aroma of freshly-brewed coffee, the gift of taste buds, the emotional outlet of singing, and the existence of laughter—they all point back to a God whose creative goodness included these in the human experience. He did not have to. But his goodness spills over with unrestrained abundance, filling every corner of creation. Because goodness is what God is, goodness is what God naturally does.

God's goodness is also displayed in his providence. He did not merely create a good world and then leave us to ourselves; he generously sustains and is intimately involved in every detail of our world. He opens his hand to satisfy the desire of every living thing and is near to all who call on him in truth (Psalm 145:16, 18). "The LORD is good to all, and his mercy is over all that he has made" (v 9).

God is good, *all the time*.

But that doesn't mean that everything in our world is good. For we also know the good world that God created has been stained with darkness. Sin vandalised God's good creation. Violence by word and hand, broken relationships and broken nations, poverty, cancer, war, hatred, and the existence of tofu all remind us that we live in a world groaning under sin's curse. Yet even evil will be forced to serve the good plan of God. Even bad things will be used by him to achieve good ends. And nowhere is this more evident than in the sufferings of Christ, as he trusted the Father on his way toward the cross.

THE TRUST OF JESUS IN GETHSEMANE

No human looks forward to suffering, and Jesus was no different. On the night before he knew he would be crucified, facing a dark night of the soul of cosmic proportions, Jesus made his way into a garden called Gethsemane. Were we to follow him there, we would see him fall on his face in earnest and agonising prayer. If we got close enough, we would notice the very pores of his face turning red with sorrow and trouble, as his perspiration speckled the ground beneath him with blood—a rare condition known as hematidrosis, where under great emotional intensity and stress the capillaries in the sweat glands rupture and mingle blood with sweat. We would hear him whisper over and over, "My Father, if it be possible, let this cup pass from me" (Matthew 26:39). What was in this dreaded cup? The unrestrained fullness of God's holy wrath poured out against my sin and yours, with a power that would make a thousand atomic explosions seem like nothing more than the hiccup of a mouse. For you and for me, Jesus drank *this* cup.

Yet on the eve of the greatest suffering the world would ever behold, Jesus exhaled the greatest seven words of trust the world would ever know: "Not my will, but yours, be done" (Luke 22:42). *Father, I trust you.* The heart of the Son found rest in the goodness of the Father. Then he got up and walked willingly into the hands of evil men with evil plans to fulfil the good plan of God.

THE GOODNESS OF JESUS AT GOLGOTHA

Because God is good, those who love him can rest in the confidence that all things will ultimately work together for *our* good, just like God promised. Nowhere is the evil-overturning goodness of God more clearly revealed than at the cross. On Golgotha—"skull hill"—God's goodness stomped on the serpent's head, just like he promised (see Genesis 3:15).

The entire life, death, and resurrection of Jesus are one continuous display of God's heart of goodness toward us. As Paul writes to Titus:

> But when the goodness and loving kindness of God our Saviour appeared, he saved us, not because of works done by us in righteousness, but according to his own mercy. (Titus 3:4-5)

Why did Jesus save me? Not because I was good but because he is good; not according to what I deserve but "according to his own mercy." That is what makes our message *good news.*

And that also means that Jesus is no stranger to our sufferings. The most natural impulse of his heart is to move toward sinners and sufferers with goodness and loving-kindness. The question is, will we trust him?

TASTE HIM TO TRUST HIM

For most of us, life has eroded away that childhood innocence in which trust was given freely and liberally. We have learned that ours is a world of broken people, who create broken structures, that offer up broken promises. Where can we discover the power to trust? David answers us from the psalms:

> *Taste and see that the LORD is good. How happy is the person who takes refuge in him! (Psalm 34:8, CSB)*

David invites us to not merely acknowledge God's goodness but to taste it. Experience it. Make our home in it. Trust toward another can only be generated by experienced goodness from another. Or as Brennan Manning put it: "You will trust [God] to the degree you know you are loved by him."[25] The cross of Christ could not declare a louder message. Like a safe harbour for a ship, like a shelter in a tornado, God's goodness toward us in Christ becomes to us a place our hearts can take refuge in. If God is good, does good, and through the work of Jesus forces even evil to work for our good, then we can trust him through every trial that comes our way.

In God's hands, even the greatest evil ever committed (the murder of Jesus), is bent backward on itself to accomplish the greatest good. The same is true for us. Like an expert judo wrestler, God's goodness in Christ takes the momentum of every painful experience in our lives, powerfully redirecting them to serve our sanctification and ultimate good.

PAIN: THE SERVANT OF MY SANCTIFICATION

None of us like pain, and only a fool goes looking for it. But neither should we be surprised when we encounter it. Paul wants us to become convinced that our afflictions actually play a role in *preparing* us for our eternal future!

> *So we do not lose heart. Though our outer self is wasting away, our inner self is being renewed day by day. For this light momentary affliction is preparing for us an eternal weight of glory beyond all comparison.*
>
> *(2 Corinthians 4:16-17)*

Paul is not minimizing our struggles; he knows them all and likely a few more on a first-name basis. What he is doing is maximizing our hope. Knowing that our afflictions are preparing us for incomparable glory means that we can be honest about our troubles without becoming morbid about them.

Think about it. Doesn't hardship serve me by exposing the hidden idols that were camouflaged into the background of my successes? Doesn't difficulty have a way of shining light on some of the nocturnal narcissism still hunting for glory from the dark corners of my heart? Doesn't disappointment work for my good by surfacing my secret entitlements? Pain is as normal to life in this world as gravity; both keep our feet on the ground. I can remember sitting under the teaching of the American pastor Thabiti Anyabwile as he walked us through the relationship between suffering and renewal. At one point he dropped this powerful image on us:

> God is as sufficient with our suffering as He is with His Son's blood. Your suffering, Christian, is your slave. Your suffering is working for you to produce "an eternal weight of glory beyond all comparison." The next time suffering comes into your room, say, "Welcome, my slave. Produce for me the glory that God has designed."[26]

ALL THINGS FOR GOOD

Measuring our present moments of difficulty by our future guaranteed eternity helps to turn anxieties into prayers and weariness into courage. In God's hands, every suffering will be forced to work for the good of his children. Every trial that rallies against us will be made to serve us. Every plan Satan devises is going to backfire on itself and accomplish the purposes of God. Every betrayal, every word of slander, every let-down, every cheap shot, every failure and late-night anxiety—all lose their power to bully us when we see them through the eternal lens of God's sovereign goodness. They are all nothing more than God-ordained servants employed in my sanctification. As Paul echoes in the timeless promise of Romans 8:28, "We know that for those who love God all things work together for good, for those who are called according to his purpose." Paul understood that even the worst parts of life were going to be used to make us gloriously like our Saviour (v 29).

So do not fear the valleys that lay ahead. Do not be surprised when the path of your life slopes downward for a time. Do not shrink back in self-pity when it seems like the shadow of darkness is getting the upper hand. The Lord Jesus will be with you in the valley (Psalm 23:4). And you can trust him. There are days coming in your future where you will find yourself opposed. That's ok. For you will never be forsaken. When you find yourself struck down, do not lose heart. Instead taste the lowliness of that moment in the company of your Saviour, and know that along with him, you can never be destroyed (2 Corinthians 4:9). Behold your God and his unswerving posture of goodness toward those who love him, and let your heart sing with the psalmist, "Surely goodness and mercy shall follow me all the days of my life, and I shall dwell in the house of the LORD forever" (Psalm 23:6). So too, meditating on God's perfect sovereignty and goodness is how you ready yourself for hard times before they arrive.

Why can we trust Jesus with the entire spectrum of what troubles us? Because the scars on his body evidence the goodness of his heart. He is weaving every dark thread of your life into a beautiful tapestry of redemption. He is recycling every one of your afflictions into the fruit of the Spirit. Not one dark day will be wasted. Our groans will be turned into glory.

REFLECTING AND APPLYING

1. Where have you personally "tasted" the goodness of God, for which you can thank him?
2. What are some ways that Jesus turns hardship into our servant? Can you remember any times that you have experienced this?
3. How might being convinced of God's goodness before hard times arrive change the way you deal with those times?

CHAPTER SEVEN

God is Love:
The Experience of
Relational Beauty

"If we do not show love to one another, the world has a right to question whether Christianity is true."
FRANCIS SCHAEFFER

"**O**nce there was a tree... and she loved a little boy."[27]
So begins Shel Silverstein's classic children's picture book, *The Giving Tree*. What follows is a parable of happiness, consumerism, and, most important of all, love. When the boy is young, the tree gives to him her leaves for a crown, her branches for him to climb, and her apples for him to enjoy. "And the boy loved the tree... and the tree was happy."

But as time goes by, the boy becomes a young man. His simple childlike enjoyment of the tree for what she was changes. Now he wants money and possessions. So the tree, loving the young man, gives him her apples to sell by the cartload. *And the tree was happy.* Years go by, and the boy-now-a-man desires a house to raise a family in, so the tree, loving him, tells him to cut off her branches and build his house. *And the tree was happy.* More years go by, and the boy comes back in his middle age wanting a boat to sail away from the monotony of life. So the tree, loving the boy, gives her trunk to him for a boat, and the boy sails away. And there she is, reduced to nothing more than a stump, left alone again. Then one day, the boy, now in the dusk of his years, returns to the tree weary from his life. All he desires now is a place to rest. And the tree, loving the boy, invites him to come sit upon her stump. *And the tree was happy.*

This profound short story shocks us—and over 50 years since it was first published, it continues to divide opinions in that most visceral of forums: Amazon reviews. Is it, in the words of one *New York Times* article, a "tender story of unconditional love or [a] disturbing tale of selfishness"? Perhaps the secret of the book's longevity lies in its ambiguity.

Yet I think the story reminds us of something that strikes at the core of existence: *to truly love is to give yourself away.* As we think back on the people who have loved us—perhaps a parent, grandparent, friend, or family member—we can't help but see that the way they loved us was in giving themselves to us. The countless moments of sleep sacrificed, dollars spent, hours given, patience extended, and encouragement poured out on our behalf. Through word and action and sacrifice, they imperfectly communicated their love to us in varying ways and with varying intensity. They showed us what we all, deep down, yearn to experience: love.

That said, we have a rather odd relationship with the word, *love*, as far as the English language is concerned. Take, for example, my love for my children. That love is powerful and intense and protective. I tell them every day, *I love you*, and that love is expressed as I serve them by giving myself to them (as the saying goes, "love" to a child is spelt T-I-M-E).

Yet I also love chicken wings. Here too, my love is deep. But that love is expressed by devouring them. A lot of them. If an observer from another world were to hear me declare my love for chicken wings and then watch that love demonstrated, followed by a declaration of my love for my kids, they would be understandably confused (and also calling Child Services!).

So let's add another descriptor of this essential human experience to our vocabulary: *relational beauty*. While we often use the word "love" to describe an admiration of a thing for what it can give us, "relational beauty" describes a powerful affection toward another that is displayed in a willingness to lay down our life for them. This second kind of love is an attribute of God himself, revealed with unmistakable fierceness in the cross of Christ. When played out horizontally in human relationships, it goes far deeper than mere emotional sentiment or fleeting romance or lustful appetite or a mere love of "love." This kind of love is active and self-giving. It is relational beauty; the way things are meant to be, because it is what God is at his very heart.

GOD IS LOVE

Among the most repeated phrases amongst Christians is a phrase taken word for word from 1 John 4:8: "God is love." This little statement is both beautifully simple and yet stunningly profound. And we can affirm it with confidence for three primary reasons.

The first reason we know that God is love is because God himself repeatedly says so. The Old Testament declares over and over that he is "abounding in steadfast love." These words, first spoken by God when he revealed his glory to Moses on Mount Sinai (Exodus 34:6), are later sung by David as the reason why he trusts in the Lord and praises him (Psalm 86:5; 103:8; 145:8). It's a phrase repeated by the prophet Joel as the basis on which God's wayward people can return to him with repentance (Joel 2:13). And it's why the runaway prophet Jonah refused to go preach to his enemies in Nineveh, because he knew that a God "abounding in steadfast love" would give them revival instead of retribution if they only turned to him (Jonah 4:2).

In the New Testament, God's sacrificial love—his *agape*

love—is mentioned an incredible 259 times. It is the marvellous gift of a holy God toward undeserving sinners, not due to any merit in them but due to the sheer magnitude of God's generous heart (Deuteronomy 7:7-8; Romans 5:8). In the words of C.S. Lewis, this is not "because we are so loveable, but because he is so loving. Not because he needs to receive, but because he delights to give."[28]

Second, God is love because God is triune. Have you stopped to wonder what God was doing *before* he created the world? What was his experience before sun and moon, land and oceans, creatures and people? Was he lonely? Bored, even? *Not at all.* God's experience of himself in eternity past was one of blazing, glorious, perfect love poured forth between the Father, Son, and Spirit. Jesus showed us this in John 17:24 when he prayed: "Father … you loved me before the foundation of the world." The Father is the source and wellspring of this triune love. The Son is the perfect expression of the triune love. The Spirit is the ever-flowing activity of the triune love.

Because God is love—and because his creation flows from his character—that means the foundation of all human reality is love. It underpins the entirety of how the universe works. If there is no God of love, then the universe is nothing more than meaningless chaos where, as author Reynolds Price writes, "senseless atoms and vicious creatures stage the awful pageants of their wills."[29] Or if there is a god, but he is not triune—as is the case in the Muslim conception of Allah—then such a divine being could not *be love*, since there would have been a time before the creation of the world where he was entirely alone. And true love can only exist in a relationship. True love has to be *given*.

Yet God is love, because God is a Trinity. God is within himself the source and perfection of all relational beauty. He has never been lonely; the Father, Son, and Spirit have been giving and receiving love in its most pure form for all eternity. And it is here, in the doctrine of the Trinity, that we actually can answer some of the most important human questions: *Why are we here? What is the meaning of life? And for heaven's sake, why would a God who already had the most potently satisfying experience of divine love within himself create the constantly grumbling, continually self-centred, cosmic headache known as humanity? Us?* "There's only one answer," writes Timothy Keller. "He must have created us not to get joy but to give it."[30]

If God is within himself a relationship of pure and undiluted beauty, and if we have been made in his image (Genesis 1:26), then he has created us to enter into that very experience; vertically with him and horizontally with others. Why did God create a world? To include us in the experience of beauty he has eternally possessed. To invite us into the divine dance. As Jesus prayed to the Father in the preceding verses of John 17:

> *[I ask] that [my people] may be one even as we are one, I in them and you in me, that they may become perfectly one, so that the world may know that you sent me and loved them even as you loved me. (John 17:22-23)*

Third, God is love because God is the most generous in his self-giving. As Silverstein helped us to see, in stark contrast to the self-absorption of the boy, love gives itself away. And to an undeserving world, God gave the most precious gift of all. *Himself.*

LOVED FROM SKY TO SKY

"For God so *loved* the world, that he *gave* his only Son, that whoever believes in him should not perish but have eternal life" (John 3:16). And Jesus didn't just give us his presence—he "loved [us] to the end" (John 13:1) by giving us his very life. He willingly allowed himself to be cut down to the stump. And here we see that the experience of relational beauty and the giving of sacrificial love are inseparably woven together. As Jesus said on the eve of his death, "Greater love has no one than this, that someone lay down his life for his friends" (John 15:13).

Can I press this truth a little deeper into your heart?

Jesus loved you to the death before there was one molecule of love in your heart toward him.

Jesus loved you to the death before you prayed one word, read one verse, or gave one cent.

Jesus loved you to the death on your worst day, not your best.

Jesus loved you to the death, knowing every hell-deserving denial of him you would ever commit before you turned to him. Along with each one after. He bore your punishment in total.

Jesus loves you with a love so mind-boggling—so "wide and long and high and deep"—that it "surpasses knowledge" (Ephesians 3:18-19, NIV). It is a love that is vaster in its breadth than all of your rebellion; more permanent in its length than the existence of the universe; supreme in its height, outranking every human and demonic accusation; and so immeasurable in its depth, that no matter how low you have fallen, his arms are deeper still. Vast, permanent, supreme, and immeasurable; we will sooner drain the oceans of our planet than the love of Christ for those who are his. As Frederick Lehman's wonderful hymn, *The Love of God is Greater Far*, expresses:

> Could we with ink the oceans fill,
> Or were the skies of parchment made;
> Were every stalk on earth a quill,
> And every man a scribe by trade;

To write the love of God above,
Would drain the oceans dry,
Nor could the scroll contain the whole
Though stretched from sky to sky.[31]

LOVE FOR A MONDAY MORNING

When asked in 1962 to sum up his life's work of theological study in a single sentence, the renowned scholar Karl Barth responded with, "Jesus loves me, this I know, for the Bible tells me so."[32] To know that you are the beloved of Jesus and have done nothing to deserve it is the cure for all our restlessness, the antidote to all our entitlement, and the preemptive counterpunch to every sinful temptation. To know that you are accepted by him through sheer grace is the remedy for every midlife crisis or Monday-morning blues, every parental moment of exhaustion, every heartbreak, every false accusation, every hurtful word of gossip, every minute of human loneliness, and every time things don't play out the way you hoped. The 20th-century minister Martyn Lloyd-Jones knew this and said:

> In one sense the whole object of being a Christian is that you may know the love of Jesus Christ, his personal love to you; that he may tell you in unmistakable language that he loves you, that he has given himself for you, that he has loved you with an everlasting love.[33]

Is there any higher privilege than experiencing the beauty of being the beloved of Jesus? To be loved with a love that is not fickle or temperamental but everlasting? A love that is not fluctuating up and down with our performance for God but unwaveringly secure in Christ's perfect life and love for us? "In this is love, not that we have loved God but that he loved us and sent his Son to be the propitiation for our sins" (1 John 4:10). Do you believe this? God will stop at nothing—not even our own folly or hostility or stupidity—to love his people undeservedly, all the way to glory.

The divine love, because it is the truest of loves, is a love that does something.

It is the prophet Hosea pursuing with unrelenting tenderness his unfaithful wife, Gomer (Hosea 1 – 3).

It is a man selling all he has that he may obtain the treasure buried in a dusty old field (Matthew 13:44).

It is Christ giving his very life to secure our place in God's family.

BEAUTY AND BELIEVABILITY

The love that Jesus gives to us is the energising power for the love he commands from us. Love is what his people are to be known by. On the night before his death, Jesus told his disciples: "Just as I have loved you, you also are to love one another. By this all people will know that you are my disciples, if you have love for one another" (John 13:34-35). The gospel doctrine of "just as I have loved you" creates a gospel culture of "love one another." The horizontal beauty displayed amongst professing Christians is a powerful argument for the reality of God. So much so that the beauty of human relationships is Christ's primary evidence for the authenticity of our faith.

In John 13:35 Jesus is connecting the believability of our message with the beauty of our relationships. More than ever before, we are living in a time where our world needs to see that the gospel story is attractive before they will consider whether or not it is true. Notice our Lord did not say that we will be known by the magnificence of our miracles or the excellence of our programmes or even the precision of our doctrine (as important as that is), but by our love for one another. The early church father Tertullian said that the pagan world of Rome looked at the Christians and exclaimed, "See how these Christians love one another, they are even ready to die for one another!" What might happen in our day if the world were to see such relational beauty demonstrated in our churches?

Paul writes in Ephesians 4:1-2:

I therefore, a prisoner for the Lord, urge you to walk in a manner worthy of the calling to which you have been called, with all humility and gentleness, with patience, bearing with one another in love.

The worthy life—the life we have been saved into through the sacrifice of Jesus—is a life marked by love. A life where we willingly follow in the footsteps of our Saviour and give our very selves to one another. Nowhere is this demonstrated more clearly than in the way we treat each other in our local churches. Churches convinced of the imperative to love become places where all the "one anothers" of New Testament Christianity become the regular felt experience in our shared life together. Forgiving, honouring, and devoting ourselves to one another becomes normal. Pretending, posturing, and standing aloof from one another becomes weird. Why? Because the love of Christ has settled in our hearts.

The presence of biblical non-negotiables like humility and gentleness and patience and love among God's people validates our gospel message. And the absence of such relational beauty in a local church vandalises our truth with an anti-gospel ugliness. In our age of perpetual outrage and theological tribalism, never has this been more important.

What if we took seriously Paul's warning to watch closely not only our doctrine but also our lives (1 Timothy 4:16), because we valued relational beauty just as highly as we valued doctrinal accuracy? What if we became utterly convinced that possession of all miraculous power and theological mystery, devoid of love, comes out as a negative in God's math (1 Corinthians 13:2)? What if those of us who hold to the doctrine of grace were as dogmatic about the presence of graciousness in our churches? What if God's people over the coming decades gave themselves to re-learning the difficult lessons of not only "neighbour-love" but "enemy-love"?

Our increasingly angry world will know that our good news is *true* news when God-reflecting relational beauty shines through in the way we treat one another. "Greater love has no one than this, that someone lay down his life for his friends" (John 15:13). We can't often honestly say that we have loved others like that; but we can always wholeheartedly say that Jesus has loved us like that. What a privilege it is, to be counted his friend.

REFLECTING AND APPLYING

1. What are some ways you have seen the presence of relational beauty in the church reinforce the message of the gospel? What are some ways you've seen its absence in the church do harm to the gospel message?

2. What happens in your heart when you see that God will stop at nothing to love his people undeservedly, all the way to glory?

3. Where in your life are you tempted to minimize the love of Jesus?

4. Where in your life are you struggling most to demonstrate relational beauty to others? How does the gospel apply to that struggle?

CHAPTER EIGHT

God is Never Late: The Experience of Patience

"Do not look sad. We shall meet soon again."
"Please, Aslan," said Lucy, "what do you call soon?"
"I call all times soon," said Aslan; and instantly he was
vanished away.
C.S. LEWIS, THE VOYAGE OF THE DAWN TREADER

We do not wait well. At least, I know I don't.

Once when I was 13 years old, my impatience got the better of me in spectacular style. Alone in my home while the rest of my family was out running errands, I could no longer stand not knowing what was on the other side of the red and gold wrapping paper that covered the array of shapes under our Christmas tree. It almost seemed as if those brightly coloured patterns were taunting me; defying me, even. And on this day, curiosity conquered self-control. Just a week away from Christmas, I unwrapped the presents under the tree with my name on them. Followed by the presents with everyone else's names on them.

Every. Single. One.

Obviously, I was not going to be caught like a family pet who has made a mess of things, and then has to wait out the remainder of the day until they inevitably face the music when their owner arrives home. Having received from my Creator the gift of opposable thumbs, I carefully re-wrapped each present to avoid rousing the suspicion and subsequent punishment from my parents.

And—it worked. I spent the entirety of that Christmas morning gasping with open mouth and feigned surprise as each gift was opened by myself and others (sorry Mum). All just to be free from that haunting spectre of uncertainty we call waiting.

ARE WE THERE YET?

It is exactly this inability to wait well that drags each of us into a pattern of life where we are perpetually in a hurry. We find ourselves always in a rush to get somewhere we're presently not, or to become someone we presently aren't. Scrolling through the smiling highlight reels of those on our Instagram feeds, we become imperceptibly driven by a sense of cosmic FOMO (fear of missing out).

Fear of missing out on whatever is coming up next.

Fear of missing out on life.

The result is an addiction to speed of the non-narcotic kind (which, by the way, is no less potent in its ability to diminish our lives). We speed through our conversations, our thoughts, our to-do lists, our decisions, our favourite Netflix series, our meals, and ultimately our lives like we're being chased by the police. We order something online and expect its arrival within days. Woe to those who casually dawdle through airports in front of us or have the audacity to drive under the speed limit in the overtaking lane! Don't people realise we have somewhere to be? And even when we're aware of this tendency, our prayers still seem to be, "Lord please make me patient... now!" Why can't God just hurry up already?

Those of us living in Western cultures are generally about as restless and impatient as a four-year-old on a cross-country road trip. "Are we there yet? How much longer?" comes the voice from the backseat of our hearts, as we barely pass the end of our street. We think to ourselves, *Once I arrive "there," then everything will be ok.* But here's the truth: the idea that we will ever be satisfied by our constant rush toward our own personally defined "there," is nothing more than a mirage. It shimmers on the horizons of our imagination, but only lures us deeper and deeper into a desert of discontentment.

Instead, we need to learn to live at the Spirit's pace. What if we learned to really understand the faithfulness of God, the perfection of his timing, and that he has never once been behind schedule?

THE GOD WHO IS NEVER LATE

In a world that shifts as constantly as the surface of the ocean, where the winds of culture may change direction at a moment's notice, God's faithfulness stands firm and true. His commitment to the fulfilment of his plans at the right time is as unwavering as Mount Everest before a desk fan. He is the eternal God; existing outside of time and uninhibited in his ability to move within it. As we saw earlier in this book, God fully inhabits not only every *where* but also every *when*. How could a God who holds time in his hands like you hold this book ever be described as "late?" Jen Wilkin summarises this perfectly:

> He is simultaneously the God of the past, present, and future, bending time to his perfect will, unfettered by its constraints. The past holds for him no missed opportunity. The present holds for him no anxiety. The future holds for him no uncertainty.[34]

God's faithfulness is described in Scripture as reaching to the skies (Psalm 36:5); as an all-surrounding reality unique to him (Psalm 89:8); and as a shield we can take refuge under (Psalm 91:4). Both the shortest and the longest chapters of the Bible remind us that God's faithfulness endures forever, to all generations (Psalm 117:2; Psalm 119:90). In a world of broken promises and betrayals, we can come home to rest in a God who is infinitely faithful in every way, in every thing, and in every age.

Another way of understanding God's faithfulness is by looking back on the track record of his promises. God the promise-maker is the perfect promise-keeper. When God speaks out a promise, he speaks out reality. God makes his faithfulness known to us through the prophet Isaiah again and again. He declares that his word, "shall not return to me empty, but it shall accomplish that which I purpose" (Isaiah 55:11). What he plans shall be, what he purposes shall stand (Isaiah 14:24). No wonder the prophet responds, "I will exalt you; I will praise your name, for you have done wonderful things, plans formed of old, faithful and sure" (Isaiah 25:1).

We know this too from our favourite stories of Scripture.

When God promised Abraham that he would make his descendants into a mighty nation…

When God promised Joseph the honour of his entire family…

When God promised Moses that he would deliver Israel from a ruthless dictator…

When God promised Hannah a child, David a kingdom, and Mary a Messiah…

… God was faithful to his promise. In David's words, "The counsel of the LORD stands forever, the plans of his heart to all generations" (Psalm 33:11).

Now that's not to say that you and I are always going to get what we want, when we want it. We need look no further than the preceding verse to be reminded, "The LORD brings the counsel of the nations to nothing; he frustrates the plans of the peoples" (Psalm 33:10). Much of our disappointment comes from an entitlement that believes God owes us anything we want, or has promised to give us something specific in our own circumstances that he never actually did. For others of us, our disappointment comes from a mindset informed more by microwaves than marathons. We just don't know how to *wait*.

To be sure, there are some figures in Scripture who received the fulfilment of God's promise instantly. Others waited for what seemed like a lifetime filled to the brim with wasted opportunities. Joseph spent nearly 14 years between his dreams and his throne. For David, it was 15 years. For others, the promise would be fulfilled in their descendants, many generations later. But on the final day, there won't be a single person standing before the throne of God who will raise their hand and say, "I think you forgot something."

What greater power is there for a life marked by patience than understanding that God has a perfect plan, that will happen at the perfect time, and that has never once been derailed by our ability to make a mess of things?

How would your life change, if you really believed that God is more patient with you than you will ever be with yourself? If you were convinced to your very core that the God who begins a work in someone has never once failed to finish what he started (Philippians 1:6)? If you knew deep down, that despite all your sin and shortcomings, he is not condescendingly tapping his watch at your pace of sanctification, ready to give up because change is taking too long. Just the opposite. God will step down from being *God* before he goes back on the promises he has made to his children. As Jeremiah points out, his love is never-ceasing, his compassion never-ending and his mercy new every morning. Why? For "great is [his] faithfulness" (Lamentations 3:22-23).

He is faithful to his purposes.

He is true to his promises.

He finishes what he started in his own good time.

He is never in a hurry.

JESUS: RIGHT ON TIME

Jesus is the full embodiment of God's faithfulness to his promises. Whenever we are tempted to wonder if God's apparent "delay" means that he has forgotten us or changed his mind, we need only look to Jesus. Paul reminds the Christians in Galatia that "when the fullness of time had come, God sent forth his Son…" (Galatians 4:4). He tells the Christians in Rome that "at just the right time, when we were still powerless, Christ died for the ungodly" (Romans 5:6, NIV). The fulfilment of God's plan to send Christ—set in motion from the very beginning—took place exactly when God intended it to. Not a day too early or a day too late. In the sending of Jesus, God shows us that he is faithful. And in the life of Jesus, we find an example of patience that delights in the Father's timing and plan.

As we read the Gospels, in Jesus we catch a glimpse of humanity that is never once in a hurry. Jesus lived patiently at the Spirit's pace, according to his Father's schedule. As a boy, he lingered at the temple in his "Father's house" (Luke 2:41-49) because it wasn't yet time to leave. Over and over, he didn't see interruptions as an inconvenience to his (or anyone else's) plans but as part of the Father's plan. Just read through the series of events in Matthew 9:18-26, where even the interruptions of Jesus' day are interrupted! C.S. Lewis drives this point home:

> The great thing, if one can, is to stop regarding all the unpleasant things as interruptions of one's "own", or

"real" life. The truth is of course that what one calls the interruptions are precisely one's real life—the life God is sending one day by day: what one calls one's "real life" is a phantom of one's own imagination.[35]

Whether it's the small, daily disruptions, or the entire year known as 2020, how do you find yourself living in the times of waiting that God ordains? If, like me, you are still in the school of patience, have you ever considered that Jesus—with a world to save, people to heal, good news to preach, and atonement to make—spent 30 years in his stepfather's trade, building Galilean furniture, covered in sawdust, learning the names of the trees? And then when it was finally time to begin his public ministry after his baptism by John, it began with… more waiting.

In a wilderness.

Being tempted by Satan.

In fact, each time Satan attempted to derail the ministry of Jesus right there in the desert, he did so with something that had to do with hurrying ahead of God's plan.

First was the hurry of immediate gratification: "Command these stones to become loaves of bread" (Matthew 4:3). Second came the temptation to prove himself with a spectacular display: *If you're really the Son of God, prove it. Throw yourself off the temple and have the angels catch you* (v 5-6). Finally, Satan baited his hook with global glory and power (v 8-9).

Each of these temptations—gratification, legitimacy, and glory—had to do with timing. Eventually Jesus' fasting would come to an end, his identity as the Messiah would be vindicated, and the glory of the kingdoms of the earth would belong to him. But not yet. And in the not-yet, Jesus patiently trusted the Father's timing.

Not once in Jesus' life do we find him in a hurry. He is simultaneously the faithfulness of God we need to remember and the patience of God we need to imitate. Jesus models for us how to embrace the tension of something that is already given but not yet completed. In Jesus, the kingdom of God has come—but is also still yet to come. God is not slow to fulfil his plans. He accomplishes them exactly as he means to.

In the Old Testament, God promised a Messiah. And Jesus came.

In the New Testament, Jesus promised he would return. And he will.

IMPATIENCE IS PRIDE

A recent word-search in my Bible of "patience/patient" showed me how painfully and frequently I had brushed over this word (how ironic). How had I missed that this was the very first word Paul chose to describe the great mega-reality of what love is like? "Love is patient" (1 Corinthians 13:4). Why did it take me so long to work out that the "worthy" life to which Jesus redeemed me, is one marked by humility, gentleness, love, and... patience (Ephesians 4:1-2)?

It is true that I am still impatient. I still eat my food too fast and receive an annual speeding ticket with the regularity of a birthday. But I am learning to slow down, and to be attentive to the Spirit's pace in my life and within our church. Increasingly I am discovering the exhilarating contentment of just being still before the Lord.

And the more I do, the more I realise that all of my impatience is really just the pride of thinking that my timing is better than God's timing. Thinking that my plan is *the* plan. Assuming that God wants my cleverness, instead of my trust. Are we so different to Israel—throwing together a golden calf of our own hurried ingenuity, instead of waiting on what can only come from the hand of God? Is it any wonder that the wisdom writings juxtapose patience with pride? "Better is the end of a thing than its beginning, and the patient in spirit is better than the proud in spirit" (Ecclesiastes 7:8). That is the kind of patience I am seeking to cultivate. Will you join me?

PATIENCE IS A (MISSIONAL) VIRTUE

In his insightfully titled book, *The Patient Ferment of the Early Church*, the historian Alan Kreider makes the case that one of the essential virtues of the early Christians living under Roman rule was patience. Since God was patient, and Jesus embodied patience, the early church determined that "they, trusting in God, should [also] be patient—not controlling events, not anxious or in a hurry, and never using forces to achieve their ends."[36] What wisdom for living! Interestingly, the first major treatise on a Christian virtue written by the church fathers was by Tertullian (around the beginning of the third century) and was called *De Patientia*—or "Of Patience." At a time when Christianity was advancing across the world despite much persecution, why a treatise on patience? Tertullian understood the subversive witness patience had in a pagan world when it became obvious in the people of God.

> It attracts the heathen ... adorns a woman, perfects a man. It is loved in a child, praised in a youth, esteemed in the aged. In both man and woman, at every age of life, it is exceedingly attractive.[37]

If we too are to penetrate this age with faithful witness, the children of a hurried world need to see something captivating in the children of God. They need to glimpse an emotionally-satisfying experience of lived Christianity in all its beauty, before they will engage with its truth claims. The gospel story needs to be seen as attractive before it will be considered true. Patience in the face of personal rejection or cultural hostility or life's inevitable hardships becomes non-ignorable. It is otherworldly. It is the evidence of a people who know they are loved, and therefore give love. It was the missional posture of the early church, who were able to absorb the worst that the Roman empire could dish out, then stand back up and invite their oppressors in for dinner.

As with a seed hidden in the ground, just because we can't see the immediate results, it doesn't mean miraculous life isn't forming. Like the gradual process of fermentation, patient living may not display the same spectacular immediacy we are so used to being wowed by in our world. But over time, it demonstrates a bubbling energy that possesses a cumulative power to bring about tremendous renewal in us and around us.

LIVING AT THE SPIRIT'S PACE

Slowing your pace, in order to increase your longevity, is a step forward in fruitfulness, not backward. In a time of great haste, we need to re-learn practices that lead us toward patience. Sure, let's pray outrageously big prayers. But what if we also embraced godly limitations through the kind of habits that lead to a faithful finish? Habits like honest friendships, where we make a point to regularly connect in an unhurried space with someone who knows us and loves us. Rhythms like weekly Sabbath rest, where our ever-buzzing phones and our ever-working brains learn to stop, be still, and simply enjoy God and the good gifts he has given us. Entering into protected times of prayer each day where we can give thanks, confess sin, plead our needs, and delight in our Father. Each of these are practices that intentionally slow us down and teach us to live at the Spirit's pace.

If God is committed to conforming Christ in us and advancing his mission through us, then we can relax into the hard-working rhythms of sowing, watering, and reaping, while leaving the results to him. Like the enduring farmer, we can learn to embrace the rhythm of seasons and the discipline of delayed gratification. As James 5:7-8 reminds us, "See how the farmer waits for the precious fruit of the earth, being patient about it, until it receives the early and the late rains. You also, be patient. Establish your hearts, for the coming of the Lord is at hand."

When things don't go according to your plans—even those plans that you believe will bring glory to God—you can rest in the truth that "the Lord is at hand." Why? Because he is faithful. And all who wait patiently for him are happy (Isaiah 30:18, CSB). God knows exactly what he is doing. He will accomplish his purposes, in his way, at just the right time. And he always keeps his word.

Repeat after me: *If God is never late, then I can wait.*

In what areas of your life do you need to yield to God's pace? In what corners of your heart are you restless or despairing? Patience grows when we remember that we don't need to see what's coming up around the bend; we just need to fix our eyes on him. Isaiah reminds us that God-renewing endurance in life comes no other way, but through beholding the Lord (Isaiah 40:31). So look at him. His promises are true, and his timing is perfect.

Do you feel overlooked by God? Have the long seasons of waiting in your life caused you to think that you have been forgotten by him?

He sees you.

He will not fail to be faithful to his purposes in your life.

The one who invented time is never behind schedule. And in that glorious truth is the power to face anything. Even waiting.

REFLECTING AND APPLYING

1. Have you ever thought about impatience in terms of pride? How does that change the way you see "hurry" in your life?

2. In what ways does remembering the faithfulness of God to accomplish his purposes empower you to "wait well"?

3. How do habits that help you slow down and embrace godly limitations—like honest friendships, Sabbath rest, unhurried prayer, or a "Rule of Life" (google *The Common Rule* by Justin Earley)—establish a marathon-runner mentality in the Christian race? What is one of these habits you can begin cultivating more intentionally this week?

4. Make a list of areas in your life that you tend to move too fast in (for example, decision-making, driving, resting, etc.). As you identify each one, think of ways you can practically slow down which will help you to be more attentive to God and others in that space.

CHAPTER NINE

God is Merciful: The Experience of Gentleness

"That God is rich in mercy means ... our haunting shame is not a problem for him, but the very thing he loves most to work with."

DANE ORTLUND

After a sentence of 19 years of hard labour for petty crimes that led him into a deepening moral darkness, an ex-convict re-enters a world which wants nothing to do with him. Despised by people, turned away by motel owners, bitten by a dog, and with nowhere to go, he eventually stumbles upon the home of an elderly bishop who gives him a place at the table, silverware to eat with, a bed to sleep on. The criminal is dignified by the kindness of the bishop, who addresses him tenderly as *my brother* and *sir*.

> Each time [the bishop] said the word *Sir* with his gentle grave voice, the man's face was illumined. *Sir* to a convict is like a glass of water to a shipwrecked sailor.

In every way possible, the posture of the bishop toward the ex-criminal is one of merciful gentleness. His voice is *gentle*. His words are *gentle*. His touch is *gentle*. His eyes are *gentle*.

To understand the contrast between the two characters is to imagine "what is most violent in the presence of what is gentlest."

How does the ex-criminal repay such a display of undeserved hospitality? He robs the godly man of his silverware, fleeing into the night. Sometime the next day, there is a knock on the bishop's door. As it opens, there stand on the doorstep several men in uniforms; one holding a bag of valuables, and two more holding none other than the ungrateful thief himself.

"We caught this man in town with this bag," begins one of the men in uniform, "and he told us that— "

"Yes, yes," interrupts the bishop, "he told you that the silverware had been given to him by a kind old priest he has passed in the night. But my friend," says the bishop turning to the thief, "why did you not take the silver candlesticks that I gave to you as well? Gentleman," continues the bishop to the others, "this is all a mistake, what this man told you is true."

The bewildered officers release an even more bewildered criminal from their custody and depart on their way. Alone together at the front door, the bishop approaches the confused criminal, and placing the candlesticks in his hands, says in a low, solemn voice, "My brother, you no longer belong to evil, but to good. It is your soul that I buy from you … and I give it to God."

The above story is of course from Victor Hugo's masterpiece, *Les Misérables*, which goes on to tell of how the criminal— Jean Valjean—becomes the new man the bishop declared he would become.[38] Here's the point: it was undeserved mercy that tenderised the hard heart of Jean Valjean. Such mercy is the bestowment of gentleness on us from someone who has every right to give us justice and whatever consequences fit our offence. Mercy changes us first by shocking us with its unexpected presence, then by dignifying us with its unexpected impact. Like the presence of a kind ruler in a prison giving out pardons, or like a letter of forgiving love to an unfaithful spouse instead of divorce papers, mercy is simultaneously jarring and gentling. It is both glorious and scandalous. It is the very heart of God.

THE GOD WHO IS RICH IN MERCY

Some people have this idea that God is a God of mercy in the New Testament, but is all fire, brimstone, and judgment in the Old Testament. But in fact, as Tozer points out, God's mercy is spoken of four times more frequently in the Old Testament than it is in the New Testament.[39] God's gracious and merciful character is an unchanging biblical constant through the historical books (Exodus 34:6; 2 Chronicles 30:9; Nehemiah 9:17), the songs (Psalm 86:15; 103:8; 111:4; 112:4), and the prophets (Joel 2:13; Jonah 4:2).

In the New Testament, Paul describes God as "the Father of mercies and God of all comfort" (2 Corinthians 1:3). Mercy is the natural offspring of his fatherly heart. He is the cause and source of all mercy, and apart from his existence, the category of human mercy is about as likely as a ravenous wolf being merciful to an injured lamb. Yet for God, mercy is not a feeling he drifts into when he is in a generous mood. It is the ever-flowing fount of the deepest part of his heart. His merciful grace shines forth from Genesis to Revelation. As David declared: "His mercy is over all that he has made" (Psalm 145:9).

Yet while mercy and grace are the closest of companions, they are not synonyms. Mercy is the *withholding* of punishment deserved; grace is the *giving* of a gift undeserved. Mercy happened when the bishop withheld the consequences of Jean Valjean's crimes; grace happened when the bishop gave him all his silverware plus an additional two candlesticks. Mercy is God's generous *not-punishing* of us; grace is God's generous

provision toward us. They are two sides to the same coin, and
God is abundantly rich in both.

Paul points this out, reminding the Christians in Ephesus of
where they came from, and how God has treated them. Like
all of us, they were "dead" in their "trespasses and sins ... sons
of disobedience ... by nature children of wrath" (Ephesians
2:1-3). Not exactly an encouraging description of humanity.
But biblical mercy isn't afraid of being honest about the extent
of our God-betraying corruption. In fact, it goes there readily,
plunging us downward into ever-increasing truth about how
woefully short we have all fallen, so that it may trampoline us
upward into ever-increasing hope in God's posture toward us.
Which is exactly where Paul goes next:

> **But God, being rich in mercy,** *because of the great love with*
> *which he loved us, even when we were dead in our trespasses,*
> *made us alive together with Christ—by grace you have*
> *been saved ... so that in the coming ages he might show* **the**
> **immeasurable riches of his grace** *in kindness toward us in*
> *Christ Jesus. (Ephesians 2:4-5, 7, my emphasis)*

The God we meet in the Scriptures is a God who is
unbelievably rich in mercy and rich in grace. We who were
dead in our sins are made alive in Christ. We who were sons
of disobedience are adopted into God's family. We who were
once children of wrath are given a new nature. All we need to
do is turn to him and admit that we are in need of it. When
Jeremiah writes that God's "mercies never come to an end;
they are new every morning" (Lamentations 3:22-23), he is
wanting us to know that there is no sin so big or so bad that
would cause him to look at his children and say, "That's it. No
more. I'm fed up with all this constant forgiving. I'm through
with you!" No, a thousand times, no! There is never coming
a day in our future where God's mercy will be used up or off
the table for anyone who comes to him seeking it. He is not a

father who scoffs at our inability, rolls his eyes at our repeated failures, or shakes his head with a disappointed sigh at the foolishness of our sin and then walks out of the room. On the contrary, it is where we are most needy and most honest about that need that his heart is most drawn to with never-failing mercy.

The "Father of mercies" ennobles us with mercy, so that we—so similar to Jean Valjean—become those who display that same mercy to others that we ourselves have received. We become gentle. We become like Jesus.

THE GENTLE CENTRE OF THE HEART OF CHRIST

Gentleness is not niceness or wimpy-ness; it is Christlikeness. In fact, it is the heart of Christ. Throughout the Gospels we get repeated insights into the words and ways of Christ; his miracles and movements. But only once do we get an inside look into the heart of Christ from his own lips. In Matthew 11:28-29, Jesus says:

> *Come to me, all who labour and are heavy laden, and I will give you rest. Take my yoke upon you, and learn from me, for I am gentle and lowly in heart, and you will find rest for your souls.*

Of all the possible qualities we might expect to find sitting in the driver's seat of Christ's heart—the centre of his entire being; the life-directing essence of who he is and what he came to do—Jesus says that at the core of who he is, is *gentleness*. The eternal Word, who in the beginning spoke the universe into being and who at the end will return with "eyes ... like a flame of fire" as King of kings and Lord of Lords (Revelation 19:12, 16), tells us that he, and he alone, *is* the gentle rest that our own restless hearts most long to come to. He most certainly is the Lion, but in a way that is profoundly Lamb-like (Revelation 5:5-6). He most certainly is the "King of glory ... the LORD, strong and mighty" (Psalm 24:8), but he is a King who sits on a throne of grace and who welcomes with tender mercy all who draw near to him. Jesus was and continues to be an oasis of gentleness for those who have been wandering around the sin-parched desert of life lived on their own terms.

Such gentleness does not stand in contradiction to the prophetic rebuke of self-righteous people or systems. When the Scriptures say that "*God* opposes the proud but gives grace to the humble" (James 4:6), that obviously includes Jesus, who strongly challenged the unrepentant hypocrisy of self-righteous religious leaders (Matthew 23) and didn't mind driving spiritual con-men and hucksters out of the temple with a whip (John 2:13-17). Yet such occasions of holy anger on behalf of those being oppressed (which we will explore more in chapter 10) were not the daily ebb and flow of Jesus' ministry but rather Spirit-powered moments of righteous confrontation. Those who were broken over their sin he embraced with life-restoring gentleness.

What about you? When you rub up against the sin of other people, how do you respond? When I examine my own heart, it strikes me that I am at my least gentle when I think I'm right, and the other person is wrong. Or just stupid. Or both. That's when I tend to treat others with frustration or contempt or condescension, rather than gentleness. The difference between myself and my Saviour could not be more stark. In my failure to show mercy I ironically find myself all the more in need of it. Yet even here, there is grounds for hope.

From an unnamed woman in John 8—who has since become famous not for the sin of adultery which she was caught in but for the scandalous tenderness with which Jesus treated her—we receive the answer to one of the most important questions we all deep down want to know. *How will Jesus deal with me in the worst moments of my life?* As the crowd gradually disperses under the weight of Jesus' challenge—that whoever is without sin should throw the first stone (v 7)—Jesus looks at her and says, "Neither do I condemn you; go, and from now on sin no more" (v 11). Did you notice the order of his statements? First he extends mercy, and only afterward does he call her to a new way of living. The former is what empowers the latter. The author Scott Sauls writes in his book, *A Gentle Answer*:

> If you reverse the order of these two sentences, if you say, "Leave your sin" *before* you will consider saying, "Neither do I condemn you," then you have ceased to speak the language of Christ, and you have ceased to reflect the heart of Christ.[40]

On the most sinful day of our lives, Jesus does not treat us with the condemnation we deserve but with unparalleled mercy that we don't deserve. To those wearied by their sin, Jesus offers his rest. Far from treating us as we deserve, all who come to him with nothing but the honesty that admits an all-out need for a Saviour, he dignifies with undeserved gentleness. The shape of his face toward sinners and strugglers who bring their brokenness to him and lay it at his feet is never a scowl or a frown. It is in this ever-willingness of Jesus to receive you that you will find the healing balm for every anxiety that plagues you.

The further I walk with Jesus in this life, the more amazing his gentleness toward me becomes in the midst of my failures. Instead of punishing me for my sins, he absorbed the sum of my debt entirely. Instead of giving me the hell I deserve, he gives me his heaven. Not one of us deserves such generosity from Jesus. Yet this is what Christianity is. The Puritan pastor Richard Sibbes answers our uncertainty with a powerful gospel-reality: "There is more mercy in Christ, than sin in us."[41]

A REVIVAL OF GENTLENESS

Gentleness may very well be the most underrated and over-needed reality amongst Christians in the world today. It's not exactly a word that is linked with impressive, high-performing people. It's not even a word we hear all that often in our daily conversations, having been relegated to the backseat of our postmodern vocabulary along with other words of times gone by like *noble* or *valiant*. Many of us would find it hard to even articulate what it means. But we certainly know what it feels like to come into contact with it. *Gentleness is the felt experience of mercy.* Like receiving a generous gift instead of a deserved lawsuit. Like walking into a surprise party when we were expecting a jail cell. Like an embrace, when we deserved a slap. So often gentleness has a surprising quality to it, because we were expecting something else.

To be treated gently is to unexpectedly collide with our distant past. It is to taste the quality of life that existed before sin ruptured the world—a quality of life that will be our never-ending future when sin is once-and-for-all removed from the world—right here in our messy present. And in that sense, to become gentle "is to become who we were meant to be; that is, to return to who we once were, in Eden."[42]

Internally, it is a gradually increasing awareness of how mercifully God has dealt with us—and continues to deal with us—because of Jesus. Externally, we discover that we are gradually becoming more tender with others. Our responses become measured; our instincts become merciful. We're less shockable and more approachable. And while such gentleness might appear arcane, I and many like me are becoming increasingly convinced that the return of such a word—and more so, the return of such a reality—may very well be the most pressing need for the Christian church in the West today.

It won't be easy. To treat one another in ways that dignify instead of demean will require the difficult yet vital exercise of empathetic listening and self-examination. Lashing out online is easy. Using belittling sarcasm is easy. Writing people off who "just don't get it" is easy. In a world of ever-increasing outrage, demonising *them*—whoever *they* are—who sit on the opposite side to my cultural preferences, my politics, my theological convictions, my non-biblical-personal-standards-for-acceptability is easy. But gentleness can become the felt experience of our Christianity when we daily remember how merciful God has been (and continues to be) toward us.

Can I confess something here? I am writing about a quality that I deeply long to see more of in my life. A quality that dazzles me by its sheer beauty when I see it in others, and frustrates me when I discover how often it is absent in my own heart. I want to be a man, a husband, a dad, a friend, and a pastor who is remembered for being gentle. For a long time in my life I wanted to be an impressive and gifted leader. But the further I walk with Jesus, the more I find myself just wanting to be a leader who leads others more like the way he leads me: with gentleness. So onward I stumble, by the Spirit's power, pushing ever-forward into a life of gentleness that I daily experience in the patient love of Jesus. Will you join me in this pursuit?

What if we were to stubbornly go before God and pray for a revival of gentleness in our time? What if we were to lovingly demand the presence of this fruit of the Spirit as a non-negotiable in Christian leaders, just like the Scriptures do (1 Timothy 3:3; 6:11)? What if we Christians took seriously the biblical imperative to live worthy of our calling "with all … gentleness" (Ephesians 4:2)? What might the world think if it observed that our speech toward one another—in the midst of disagreements—was unmistakably flavoured with a gentleness that could only have come down from above? If mercy and forgiveness and tenderness and the benefit-of-the-doubt became so normalised in our churches that no one who was seeking rest in Jesus ever had anything to fear?

In our harsh world, gentleness is like a cool breeze on a scorching summer day. In our age of perpetual outrage, gentleness is like a soothing song, able to speak the truth to another in ways that don't strip them of dignity. To be gentle in a world of getting owned and getting even is to recreate a little corner of Eden, for "a gentle tongue is a tree of life" (Proverbs 15:4). To enter into an experience of gentleness with another is to experience life as it was meant to be, and one day will be again forever. If it changed a criminal to have a bishop call him "Sir", how much more so a sinner to have a Saviour call us "Beloved"? We only need remember that he has.

REFLECTING AND APPLYING

1. Have you met anyone who exudes the gentleness described in this chapter? What did you notice about them?

2. If a culture of gentleness were to be obvious in your church, what do you think you would see more of? What would you see less of?

3. Where or with whom do you struggle most to display gentleness?

4. How does remembering God's mercy toward us in Christ produce in us the gentleness we most desire to display?

CHAPTER TEN

God is Just:
The Experience of
Prophetic Advocacy

*"A church that does not exist to ... destroy error, to put down
falsehood, a church that does not exist to take the side of the
poor, to denounce injustice and to hold up righteousness, is a
church that has no right to be."*
CHARLES SPURGEON

can't breathe.

These three words—gasped from the lips of George Floyd
while he died under the knee of someone who had taken an
oath to "protect and serve"—reverberated around the world
in 2020. Regardless of your political view on the ensuing
aftermath or the way forward for race relations in the US, I
am sure that nearly all of us were in shocked-agreement as
we watched the sheer awfulness of a man's life being slowly
suffocated from him in the street. It was helplessness in high-
definition, immortalised with three despairing words. They
caught the attention of the public—being emblazoned across
headlines and chanted at rallies—because they resonated with
the experience of countless others who have felt "under the
knee"—whether literally or metaphorically.

I can't breathe.

Perhaps there is no better phrase to accurately capture the hopelessness experienced by those who are exploited unjustly, oppressed by the powerful, trapped by an abuser, or being wrongly held down against their will by an unjust person or system.

I can't breathe.

It is the unseen yet ever-sensed ghost that daily haunts the poor, the political refugee, and the fatherless alike. It is the unformed cry of the defenceless child being forcibly removed from the womb into an abortion clinic. It is the plea of the vulnerable that makes Triune blood boil with righteous anger on behalf of all who experience injustice. Consider the famous words God spoke to his people through the prophet Amos:

> *I hate, I despise your feasts,*
>   *and I take no delight in your solemn assemblies …*
> *Take away from me the noise of your songs;*
>   *to the melody of your harps I will not listen.*
> *But let justice roll down like waters,*
>   *and righteousness like an ever-flowing stream.*
>   *(5:21, 23-24)*

At the core of God's very essence is a burning heart of justice. So when passion in our worship is absent of a corresponding compassion toward those in need around us, God is not rightly worshiped. Or more bluntly: where God is praised vertically, but injustice is tolerated horizontally, God plugs his ears. For "just" is *who God is*, just as intensely as love, goodness, or holiness is who God is.

What is justice? Simply defined, justice means restoring *right* to the places where *wrong* is triumphing. The theologian Herman Bavinck further expanded this definition. He wrote that living justly means "not perverting [what is] due to the poor, not slaying the innocent and righteous, not accepting bribes, and not oppressing the alien, the widow, and the orphan," but rather "helping and saving the needy, who are now being ignored and oppressed and call in vain for justice; in having pity on the poor; and in redeeming their life."[43]

Therefore, a normal part of the Christian experience for all who understand that God is just and loves justice is something I will call *prophetic advocacy*. Prophetic, meaning we speak forth rightly and courageously as heralds of God's heart. Advocacy, meaning we do so on behalf of those whose cries have been ignored and whose humanity has been diminished. Beholding God's justice produces in us a desire for the same; it causes us to want what he wants; and chiefly, it compels us to act. Prophetic advocacy means we willingly enter into necessary conflict, as gentle ambassadors of the good and the true. Prophetic advocacy means we lean in, listen well, speak up, give freely, sacrifice gladly, and stand in the gap wherever we see a disconnect between God's word and oppressive realities in our world.

GOD THE JUST JUDGE

Promoting the idea of God as Judge is not exactly included among the top tips for *How to Win Friends and Influence People*, but that didn't stop the writers of both the Old and New Testaments.

Isaiah tells us that "the LORD is a God of justice" (Isaiah 30:18), and later through the same prophet, God declares, "For I the LORD love justice; I hate robbery and wrong" (61:8). The psalms constantly confirm that God is a King who loves justice (Psalm 33:5; 37:28; 99:4) and that his throne is the foundation of all justice (Psalm 9:7; 89:14; 97:2). "All his ways are justice" (Deuteronomy 32:4), which means that God is not acting in accordance with an external standard of "rightness" that exists outside of him; he is the standard. For him to act—in any way—is to act justly. When all is brought into the light before the Judge on the final day

(1 Corinthians 3:12-15; Revelation 20:11-15), there will be no doubt about the accuracy of his judgments. He will not overlook wrongs nor over-punish them. He will show neither apathy nor excess. He will judge truly. He can do no other.

JUSTICE FOR THE VULNERABLE

The Hebrew word most frequently used for "justice" or "righteous judgments" is *mishpat*, which means to give people what they are rightly owed, whether that means justifiable consequences or compassionate care. This word *mishpat* is used not only to describe God's actions but also how God calls his people to serve the vulnerable, the fatherless, the displaced, and the poor—all of whom are the most likely people in any society to find themselves "under the knee." God's heart toward each of these is so oriented toward their protection that he commands:

> *Render true judgments, show kindness and mercy to one another, do not oppress the widow, the fatherless, the sojourner, or the poor, and let none of you devise evil against another in your heart. (Zechariah 7:9-10)*

Consider the way that God describes himself in relation to each of these groups. He is "a father to the fatherless, a defender of widows" (Psalm 68:5, NIV). He is the welcoming protector of those who have been displaced (Deuteronomy 10:18; Psalm 146:9); a refuge and rescuer for the poor and the oppressed (Psalm 9:9; 12:5; 35:10; Isaiah 25:4) because they are precious to him (Psalm 72:14). If God postures himself so tenderly and protectively toward the weak of this world, how can we not do likewise?

In the same way that our face hardens and fists clench at the sight of a bully pushing around someone smaller than them, few things call forth God's holy wrath and righteous judgment like oppression of the weaker among our communities. Such wrath is "not an emotion that flares from time to time, as though God had temper tantrums," writes the author Fleming Rutledge. Instead "it is a way of describing his absolute enmity against all wrong and his coming to set matters right."[44] Does such a description of God's heart sound alien to you? While a just God of righteous judgment may grate on the sensitive ears of middle-class types like me who grew up in relative safety, to the oppressed, it is the triumphant sound of hope and vindication. As author Scott Sauls makes clear, "To accept that God is a God of love but not a judge, is a luxury that only the privileged and protected can enjoy."[45]

God stands fiercely opposed to every kind of injustice, and one day he will bring it to an end. He says to us through Isaiah:

> *Woe to those who make unjust laws,*
>   *to those who issue oppressive decrees,*
> *to deprive the poor of their rights*
>   *and withhold justice from the oppressed of my people,*
> *making widows their prey*
>   *and robbing the fatherless.*
> *What will you do on the day of reckoning?*
>   *(Isaiah 10:1-3, NIV)*

Here is something we can count on about God: no one is getting away with anything. On the day of reckoning he will set every wrong, right.

And in that truth, we have a foundation for all Christian advocacy. Because God is in the corner of the defenceless, we should make our home there too. Just like Jesus did and continues to do.

JESUS AND THE MARGINALISED

If the Old Testament left us with any doubts about God's heart for justice and our responsibility to *do justice*, the New Testament silences all excuses by putting this attribute of God in high resolution through the example, teaching, and sacrifice of Christ. Have you ever noticed how Jesus seemed to move toward the socially outcast, the politically dubious, the morally scandalous, and the physically disadvantaged on the margins of society? This solidarity of Christ with those we tend to overlook is particularly noticeable throughout the Gospel of Luke.

In Luke 1 and 2, Christ comes into the world through the womb of an unwed teenager in a rural out-of-the-way town called Bethlehem. The initial witnesses-turned-worshipers were not the powerful or the elite, but lowly shepherds, who lived on the outskirts of society. In Luke 4:18-19, Jesus preaches his first sermon, in which he announces from Isaiah that he has been anointed to proclaim good news to the poor, sight to the blind, and liberty to the captives and those who are oppressed. In Luke 5 and 6, he moves toward the physically disadvantaged with healing, and pronounces blessings on the poor, hungry, weeping, and persecuted, along with woes upon the rich and socially comfortable. In Luke 7 – 9, he is magnetised toward those who have been overlooked. He has a reputation of being a friend of sinners (7:34) and he sets those bound by demonic spirits free (8:26-39; 9:37-43).

Then in Luke 10, we encounter some of Jesus' most famous words, spoken in reply to an upstart religious expert and now known as "the greatest commandment": "Love the Lord your God with all your heart and with all your soul and with all your strength and with all your mind, and your neighbour as yourself" (v 27). The religious leader—apparently in the mood for being on the receiving end of Jesus' ultimate parable mic-drop—"desiring to justify himself, said to Jesus, 'And who is my neighbour?'" (v 29).

Cue the famous story of the Good Samaritan (it's in Luke 10:25-37 if you want to read through it again). But notice the scribe's posture in verse 29, that prompted this parable: "desiring to justify himself." It is here we glimpse the all too common pattern still present today: those who do not obey God's repeated commands to "do justice" instead seek to *justify themselves*. Instead of moving toward his neighbours with sacrificial love, this religious leader was looking for loopholes that would allow him to keep the broken world at arm's length. Can you relate? In the context of God's love for horizontal justice, isn't self-justification (defending myself) one of the clearest indicators that my heart is not in step with the heart of Christ?

In the story that follows, Jesus calls us to follow him into the fray; to move toward the margins as agents of healing and heralds of good news, without ever sacrificing one for the other. We don't cross over to the other side of the road; we enter into the hurt. And like the Good Samaritan, we offer our protection, healing, kindness, presence, and finances, along with a readiness to come back and do it all again and again with cheerful perseverance.

And this stance of Jesus toward the lowly and forgotten continues throughout Luke's Gospel: he tells parables of lost sheep and coins, prodigal sons, and persistent widows. He declares that the kingdom belongs to children. He has dinner in the home of a social traitor like Zacchaeus, and by this very act of merciful welcome, Zacchaeus is reborn and becomes a man of justice. Have we? Or have we—like the herb-tithing yet justice-neglecting Pharisees (Matthew 23:23)—marginalised the outworking of justice, instead of following Jesus into the margins as outworkers of justice? To be clear, seeking justice is not synonymous with the centrality of the gospel. But to Jesus, it is the indisputable evidence that he is in fact central to us (Matthew 25:31-46).

DEFENDING THE IMAGO DEI

As our lives are increasingly digitalised away from real face-to-face interactions, and our society becomes gradually ever-more disconnected, one of the casualties is the doctrine of *imago Dei*. This little Latin phrase comes with cosmic implications; every person you meet is made "in the image of God" and therefore is worthy of value and dignity and life. We first find it in Genesis 1:26-27 where God says, "Let us make man in our image, after our likeness." When sin entered the world in Genesis 3, it separated us from God as well as one another, staining our *imago Dei* yet in no way erasing it.

And here is where this matters: injustice increases to the degree that our understanding of *imago Dei* decreases. Isn't the absence of this the basis of all our horizontal neglect, suspicion, and hatred? Wasn't the normalisation of race-based chattel slavery during the 16th-19th centuries the result of dehumanisation—where Black men and women were recategorized as property rather than people? Weren't the genocides of Jewish people of Europe during the 1930s-1940s and the Tutsi people of Rwanda during the 1990s catalysed by the taking away of their humanity and replacing it with the labels of "rats" and "cockroaches"? In fact, the Nazis were even more explicit, describing Jews as *Untermenschen*—literally, "subhuman." Here lies the foundation of all injustice. And here lies the location of all prophetic advocacy. When *they* are not fully human but a foetus; when *they* are not human but immigrants; when *they* are not human but [insert the other political party who you loathe]; when *they* are not human but "them," it is in those spaces that Christians raise their voices with prophetic advocacy on the grounds of their *imago Dei*.

Practically then, here are three ways we can apply this and live as defenders of human dignity.

1. GIVE YOUR EARS (EMPATHIZE)

Prophetic activism begins with listening to the cries for justice around us, rather than minimising them. Empathy is a posture that seeks to understand. It means we willingly enter into the sorrows of others, being "quick to hear [and] slow to speak" (James 1:19). The gospel tunes our ears to the frequency of God's justice, so that injustice now sounds to us like a screeching violin. When someone says, "we suffer," we don't look away. We lean in. "Whenever these two words are uttered," writes Scott Sauls, "the gospel demands open ears and open hearts. The gospel demands careful, humble, non-defensive listening to the history and wounds beneath the words."[46] The Christian response to professed pain from any person—but particularly those who are socially, economically, racially, circumstantially, or relationally in a position of vulnerability—is always one of empathetic listening, not self-excusing defensiveness. It asks questions. *Tell me more. Help me understand. Help me to see.* Then we close our mouths and listen.

2. GIVE YOUR VOICE (ADVOCATE)

After we empathise, God's justice requires that we advocate. We courageously speak up on behalf of those whose voices have been drowned out. Proverbs 31:8-9 (NIV) commands us to...

> *Speak up for those who have no voice,*
> *for the justice of all who are dispossessed.*
> *Speak up, judge righteously,*
> *and defend the cause of the oppressed and needy.*

We are to speak up for the voiceless child in the womb, the voiceless woman trapped in the destructive secrecy of abuse, and the voiceless neighbour experiencing unjust treatment by those who wrongly apply their authority.

In recent years it has become theologically vogue in some quarters of Western Christianity to label those who speak up for the horizontal dimensions of justice as "cultural Marxists," as though the recognition of concepts such as power, oppression, and equal treatment originated from the corrosive atheism of Karl Marx, rather than the biblical preaching of Isaiah and the rest of the prophets. If that's the critique you fear, simply remember this: your mandate to "seek justice, correct oppression" (Isaiah 1:17); "do justice" (Micah 6:8); "establish justice" (Amos 5:15); "defend the rights of the poor and needy" (Proverbs 31:9) and confront hypocritical partiality to the rich and powerful (James 2:1-9) comes down to you from above. Such prophetic advocacy is the megaphone of God used by prophets of old to awaken slumbering consciences. It is the anchor that keeps us from drifting away into a sea of self-absorbed comfort. It is the compass that redirects the priorities of the already-justified-in-Christ back to what most deeply matters to the God of justice.

3. GIVE YOUR STRENGTH (INCARNATE)

Finally, and very importantly, God's justice requires that we take meaningful, righteous action. The application of this will vary widely depending on the context you live in, but don't miss the obvious. The prophet Micah makes clear that horizontal justice is not something we are to merely reflect on, ponder, or lament over its absence; it is something we *do*. "Do justice" (6:8). In other words, work for flourishing in all its forms, everywhere it is absent. Give generously. Prayerfully consider foster care or adoption. Do the research and find healthy organisations in the community you can partner with in practical ways. Paul instructs Titus: "Let our people learn to devote themselves to good works for pressing needs, so that they will not be unfruitful" (Titus 3:14, CSB). Commenting on this, Dr. Eric Mason explains:

> Paul sees meeting pressing needs as a core Christian commitment; not a peripheral one. We do not substitute proclaiming for action; and we don't proclaim and

neglect action. We proclaim and engage in activism that flows from the gospel.[47]

The justified are to live justly and love justice. Don't be overwhelmed by the size of the problem or discouraged that you cannot fix everything. Instead, prayerfully begin with one area of brokenness in your community. And there, give yourself to making right what is wrong with the strength that only God can provide.

THE KINGDOM REVEALED

When we turn to the present social conditions, it is not difficult to see that a great revolution is taking place. There is emerging a multitude of the neglected, demanding recognition, justice, and human rights. A new cry is heard today. The cry not only pierces the halls of government, but echoes like a wail in our churches. It is the cry of those who are awakening to a sense of bitter wrong and of social discontent. As crude as their cry may be, it is valid. People are coming to the recognition that the poor and deprived are men and women made in the image of God, thus having value ... The Church is not on the eve of destruction. It is on the eve of a revival. Like the day that comes when the long night is over, so every revival comes after times of tribulation. Nothing in the world is more certain than this. The question is not "if," but "when."[48]

The above words were written in 1909 by a Scottish author named James Burns, whose book is considered a classic on revival. They have never been more timely. Amongst the many other elements of revival (such as gospel preaching, conviction over sin, repentance, joy, openness, humility and the like), Burns identifies a renewed desire for justice and the defence of the *imago Dei* as indicators that the Spirit is at work. What if Burns was right? What if in our time we are on the edge of a spiritual sound barrier, and the social shakings around us are actually the final, jarring rattles before the sonic boom of revival?

So here's what I'm praying. I'm praying that the tensions and cross-pressures we are experiencing in the 21st century are not the *end* but an *eve* of great renewal. I'm praying that we will respond to the cries around us with a renewed commitment to the empathy and justice that God desires from us, even as I pray that he would pour out his Spirit upon our land in unimaginable ways. May he do it. And may we not lose heart. For when Jesus returns—*and he most assuredly will*—he will bring with him the perfect peace, justice, and wholeness that all of creation is groaning for. He will destroy all destruction, exile all loneliness, bankrupt all poverty, bury death once and for all, and damn hell itself. He will complete the works of his people and right every wrong with total finality. And on that day, we will behold that God's kingdom *has* indeed come, on earth as it is in heaven.

Yet until that day, we can press on with certainty with what he desires of us:

> *What does the LORD require of you*
> *but to do justice, and to love kindness,*
> *and to walk humbly with your God? (Micah 6:8)*

REFLECTING AND APPLYING

1. Where in the world do you notice an absence of the *imago Dei* being applied?

2. How does understanding Jesus' posture toward the marginalized reshape your own posture to those on the margin where you live?

3. What are some areas around you where injustice is prevailing and to which you can begin to give your ears, your voice, and your strength?

CHAPTER ELEVEN

God is Happy:
The Experience of Delight

"I saw more clearly than ever, that the first great and primary business to which I ought to attend every day was, to have my soul happy in the Lord."
GEORGE MÜLLER

Ask someone in a church to list off as many attributes of God as they can, and chances are, "God is happy" won't make it into their top twelve, if it makes the list at all. We readily (and rightly) identify that God is *holy* or that God is *love* or that God is *sovereign*. But in a way that is equally vital for a rightly shaped Christianity, we must learn to see that God is *happy*. This means that he has designed us in such a way that our walk with Jesus through a world riddled with pain and sin and suffering is simultaneously a journey in which we experience joy and pleasure and delight. If we were created for God, then we have been created for gladness. How could it be otherwise?

Think about it. Not only did God create the glorious greens and sparkling blues of places like Switzerland or Seattle in the summertime; he also gave us eyes to enjoy these colours. Not only did God create rhythm and melody and harmony; he gave us ears to delight in song and voices that we may join in. From the happy God comes every good gift contained within the human experience (James 1:17). Beauty and comedy; friendship and intimacy; playfulness and rejoicing; gladness and giggling; the rush of adrenaline and the contentment of rest; along with every delicious taste, scent, and sound—all of these exist for our enjoyment because a happy God willed them so.

Why is it so important that we see this? Why is it essential to a healthy Christianity to be convinced of the happiness of God? Because how we perceive a person's demeanour determines how we will hear their words. Take, for example, the statement "Come here." Without any context it seems to have a fairly straightforward meaning: *approach the person speaking.* But now consider how differently that simple statement is interpreted, based on the disposition of the speaker. If they are scowling with fierce eyes and a furrowed brow, "Come here" may mean a threat of violence or a scolding from a superior. Yet if the speaker is smiling from ear-to-ear, those exact same words can be the call of a loving parent wanting to embrace their child or the intimate invitation of a lover.

How you picture God when he speaks to you through the Scriptures profoundly matters. It is the difference between thinking you're hearing from a "God" who wants you to change your life so that he can stand being around you, and a God who wants to embrace you so that your delight in him increasingly changes your life. It's the difference between the rotten stench of moralism and the fragrant aroma of the gospel. And this gospel is what the prophet Isaiah calls "good news of happiness" (Isaiah 52:7), because it declares to us not the works we must do to make God happy but the works of a happy God on our behalf, so that his people may be happy in him.

IS GOD REALLY HAPPY?

Some of us may not be so sure. We're a little suspicious of the word "happiness" as a descriptor for God. But the question we want to consider is, "Who or what is the essence of happiness?" Or to phrase it another way, "Is anyone or anything happier than God is?"

The God we meet in the Scriptures is a God who, the prophet Zephaniah reminds us, rejoices over his people with gladness and loud singing (Zephaniah 3:17). Jesus tells us in Luke 15:10 that "there is joy before the angels of God" every time a wandering sinner repents and comes home. That verse isn't about angels rejoicing (though I'm sure they do); it's about the joy of whoever is before the angels. And who is it that is *before* all of heaven's angels? It is God himself. It is God the Father who celebrates the hardest and rejoices the loudest in salvation! God is far happier than we ever realised.

So too the God of the Bible takes pleasure in all that he has made. Proverbs 8 gives us a backstage, behind-the-scenes look into the original raw and unedited footage of the creation that we read about in Genesis 1. It personifies wisdom as a "master workman," who bears a striking resemblance to "the Word" described in John 1—that is, Christ. But notice *how* Father and Son go about the work of creation:

Then I [wisdom] was beside him, like a master workman, and I was daily his delight, rejoicing before him always, rejoicing in his inhabited world and delighting in the children of man. (Proverbs 8:30-31)

Proverbs 8 wants us to see the glorious happiness of the triune God, spilling out to produce the beauty of a universe. In fact, the word "rejoicing" in the above verses can also be translated as "laughing, being merry, playing." Now, how does that change the way we read Genesis 1? "In the beginning, God created the heavens and the earth" (Genesis 1:1). And as he did—as the Father, Son, and Spirit were designing and calling forth all that is—the triune God *delighted*.

BLESSEDNESS = HAPPINESS

In his wonderful books, *Happiness* and *Does God Want Us to Be Happy?*, author Randy Alcorn explains something that many of us miss when we read the word *blessed*. Consider the following handful of verses:

- "Blessed is the one whose transgression is forgiven" (Psalm 32:1).
- "Blessed is the one who trusts in you" (Psalm 84:12).
- "Blessed is the one who finds wisdom" (Proverbs 3:13).
- "Blessed is the one who fears the Lord always" (Proverbs 28:14).

Alcorn points out that for centuries after the publication of the King James Version of the Bible in the 17th century, *blessed* and *happy* were understood to be synonyms.[49] The Hebrew word translated as "blessed" in all the above Scriptures is the word *asher*, which means "happy." Either word is an appropriate translation, but only if our understanding of the word "blessedness" includes happiness explicitly within its definition! Now how does that understanding of "blessed" stoke our internal fires of delight, in the way we read those same sentences? *Happy* is the one whose sins are forgiven; *happy* is the one who trusts in you; *happy* is the one who finds wisdom; *happy* is the one who fears the Lord always. The problem isn't with the word *blessed*; the problem lies in our numbness to such a commonly heard and casually used word. Our understanding needs to be re-infused with the fullness of its biblical meaning.

In the New Testament, the apostle Paul writes to his protégé Timothy of "the gospel of the glory of the *blessed* God" (1 Timothy 1:11). Here, Paul uses the Greek word *makarios*, which also translates as—you guessed it—*happy*. No wonder Charles Spurgeon—commenting on this verse— said that the gospel is "the gospel of happiness," and that a better translation of 1 Timothy 1:11 would be "the glorious gospel of the happy God."

God, at his core, is the happiest being in the universe. And if we want further evidence, we need look no further than the person of Jesus, in whom "the entire fullness of God's nature dwells bodily" (Colossians 2:9, CSB), including the fullness of his divine happiness.

JESUS IS THE HAPPIEST PERSON IN THE UNIVERSE

Many of us have grown up with a distorted picture of Jesus as being somewhat detached from the reality inhabited by the rest of us normal mortals; an aloof ascetic who was perpetually sighing with mild disappointment at his followers. It is true that in Isaiah 53:3 he is referred to as the man of sorrows. But we must remember that Isaiah 53 is explicitly referring to the coming Messiah's suffering for us on the cross. That title is not a general description of Christ's every day but a specific description of his *final* day. Jesus is the embodiment of the happy heart of God. As John Piper writes:

> Jesus Christ is the happiest being in the universe.
> His gladness is greater than all the angelic gladness
> of heaven. He mirrors perfectly the infinite, holy,
> indomitable mirth of his Father.[50]

So if, like me, you grew up with this vision of a holy Jesus who was not necessarily a happy Jesus, then I want you to become convinced that the biblical portrait of Jesus—amongst all his other attributes—includes his happiness. If Jesus was fully and perfectly human, then isn't it reasonable to think that this included a fully and perfectly human emotional life—including happiness? It is significant that Jesus was slandered with a reputation for being "a glutton and a drunkard, a friend of tax collectors and sinners" (Matthew 11:19). If Jesus was constantly being invited to feasts and weddings and parties, surely it *wasn't* because he was known as a constant killjoy? No, it was because to be in his presence was to experience life as we were meant to know it.

And though he suffered on a Galilean hill under the weight of the sins of the world in ways we will never be able to truly comprehend, three days later he rose from the grave in glorious resurrection and later ascended to the right hand of the Father, into the same fullness of life that will one day be ours forever as well. In Psalm 16:11, David prays:

> *You make known to me the path of life;*
> *in your presence there is fullness of joy;*
> *at your right hand are pleasures forevermore.*

Where is it that we will find the maximum capacity of joy? In God's presence. Where is it that we can locate the pleasures of happiness that will never run out? At God's right hand. There is an important connection here between the "pleasures forevermore" at God's right hand, and what is described in the New Testament as occupying that very location. Think about it. What exactly is it, that we are told again (Matthew 26:64), and again (Mark 14:62), and again (Acts 2:33; 7:55), and again (Romans 8:34), and again (Colossians 3:1), and again (Hebrews 1:3; 8:1; 10:12; 12:2), and again (1 Peter 3:22), that is at the right hand of God? What would we find should we discover these "pleasures forevermore"? The answer is not a *what* but a *who*. It is Jesus himself, at the right hand of the Father.

This Jesus—the delighting, life-renewing friend of sinners— invites us daily to make our home in him. To enjoy him and be loved by him as we walk with him through every blessing and beat-down that comes our way. To be convinced that we can indeed experience the happiness we most long for in this lifetime, even if the fullness of it is still yet to come. To become a people who don't sabotage our joy by marginalising him but who solidify it by learning in every circumstance we face to "rejoice in the Lord" (Philippians 3:1).

LEARNING TO DELIGHT IN EVERY SEASON

Every person in the world is pursuing happiness, because deep down we know that happiness is something we have been created for; something we once knew and long to return to. But our efforts at chasing happiness are not working. Western culture is more technologically advanced and socially connected than at any point in human existence, and at the same time, tragically more lonely, anxious, depressed, and self-medicating than ever before. Our problem is not in a desire for happiness but in the broken places that we go looking for it. We go searching to satisfy our thirst in dirty puddles, when God invites us to drink from the river of life (Revelation 22:1).

No one knew this better than the fourth-century church father, Augustine of Hippo (Hippo being a city in North Africa, not the weirdest team mascot ever). Augustine was a young man with super-genius tendencies who spent the first part of his life chasing happiness in all the usual places of sensual pleasure. In his memoir *Confessions*, he admits having prayed, "God make me pure, but not yet!" He later turned to knowledge and rigorous self-discipline, restlessly seeking after satisfaction. Then in his early thirties, the love of God broke into his heart while reading a friend's Bible, his eyes were opened to the one place where lasting joy could be found, and his heart came alive to Jesus. He discovered that to pursue God and to pursue unfading happiness were one and the same. Reflecting on all his searching, Augustine would later write:

> There is a joy that brings true happiness, but it is not given to the ungodly. It is only for those who love You for Your own sake. That joy is to know You as You are.

This is the happy life, to rejoice in You, of You, and for You.[51]

Some Christians are serious about everything in their life, except their joy. What if we Christians really caught hold of the rejoicing heart of God and decided to go all-in as a delighting, rejoicing, celebrating people? What if we became as committed to cultivating real and deep and lasting happiness, as we were committed to pursuing holiness?

Did that last sentence jar you a little? Some of us have heard preachers make statements like, "God is not concerned with your happiness but your holiness." And yet despite their good intentions, such preachers are wrong. It should come as no surprise to any of us that God has the capacity to care about multiple parts of our lives. The biblical answer to the question, "Should we seek after holiness or happiness," is a resounding, *yes!* The God who is both happy and holy commands our rejoicing as much as he does our repenting. For what is on the other side of real repentance but a renewed gladness and joy in our salvation? Have we forgotten that the people of God who mourn over their sins also get to dance over Christ's complete and utter conquering of them? The famed British pastor of the 20th century Martyn Lloyd-Jones wrote of the early church, "What conquered the ancient world was this joy, this gladness, this verve, this indestructible quality in the life of these people, and this is the greatest need in the world today."[52]

HOW WE CAN BE THE HAPPIEST PEOPLE IN THE WORLD

In his letter to the Philippians, Paul mentions joy and rejoicing 16 times in just four short chapters. What is most remarkable, however, is that his letter is written from the inside of a jail cell. It's Paul's way of helping us to see that rejoicing and suffering are not opposites or mutually exclusive. In the normal Christian life, these two realities often co-exist at the same time. Our rejoicing isn't a naive denial of the trials of life in a broken world or a happy-clappy-glass-half-full brand of optimism. We can only rejoice in our ever-changing circumstances when our rejoicing is grounded in our never-changing Saviour, who lived, died, and rose again to give us everlasting life. No wonder Paul commands, "Rejoice in the Lord always; again I will say, rejoice" (Philippians 4:4). No wonder he can write that our lived experience is one that is often "sorrowful, yet always rejoicing" (2 Corinthians 6:10). No wonder Christians down through the centuries have been able to stare death in the face and sing.

Here's how we can truly become the happiest people in the world: we quit the pursuit of happiness as the rest of the world defines it. We stop aiming at the shadows, and we set our eyes on the reality. We fix our gaze on something even higher, and our appetite on something infinitely more satisfying. Like Augustine, we must point our hearts at nothing less than happiness in God himself.

You were made to experience delight first of all in God—the source of all happiness—who gives good gifts to enjoy as an overflow of his own glad and generous nature. When you discover the greater joy that comes when you "delight yourself in the LORD" (Psalm 37:4), you'll be able to receive all or none of the other delights of this world in ways that neither idolise them, despise them, nor despair over their absence in any given season of your life.

How do we become happy Christians? Perhaps we need to take a leaf out of George Müller's book, and learn to get our hearts "happy in the Lord." Müller was a man who founded several orphanages and dozens of schools in the 19th century; at any one time he was caring for over 1,000 orphans. Yet day by day, this was his discipline. "The first great and primary business" to which Müller applied himself each morning was to "get [his] soul into a happy state" through meditation on God's word.[53] What if you did the same? What if you refused to close your Bible in the morning without finding a reason to rejoice? What if you began to practice the art of delighting in every gift of his that comes your way—in creation, in friendship, in beauty, in taste, or a thousand other things—so that exhaling gratitude became as normal as exhaling another breath?

The message of Christianity is not, "Don't seek happiness." The message that rings out from the depths of the gospel is that in the person of Jesus, in the wisdom of Jesus, and on the way with Jesus, you'll discover the happiness your heart most deeply longs for. "May it be said of us," concludes Randy Alcorn, "that because of the happy God we know, the Jesus we love, the gospel we embrace, and the treasure we gladly share, we are truly the happiest people in the world."[54]

REFLECTING AND APPLYING

1. How does understanding the happiness of God change the way you approach him?

2. What happens when we attach our delight primarily to God's good gifts, but not to himself as the Giver? How does delighting ourselves first in God actually free us to receive his gifts with genuine happiness?

3. How might you practically take George Müller's counsel and get your heart "happy in the Lord" this week?

CHAPTER TWELVE

God is Victorious:
The Experience of Hope

Newspaper Reporter: "Sir, I understand you recently became a
Christian. May I ask you one question?"
G.K Chesterton: "Certainly."
Newspaper Reporter: "If the risen Christ suddenly appeared at
this very moment and stood behind you, what would you do?"
G.K Chesterton [looking him square in the eye]: "He is."

Eight months out of the year, I enjoy watching NBA basketball. My wife grew up in the San Francisco Bay area, so naturally we are a Golden State Warriors family. One year, during the deciding game of one of the playoffs, the game fell on a Sunday during a service, so my plan was to stay off the internet while I was teaching all day, and to watch it with Kristina later that evening. Except on this particular occasion, a man who had recently met Jesus and been baptised in our church—who we will call "D'Arcy" (for that is his name)—caught me by surprise after the service and blurted out, "Hey bro, did you catch that Warriors win today?! That Steph Curry was on fire!"

My face fell. His eyes went wide. And as the magnitude of his crime dawned on him, we both paused under the sorrowful weight of the moment, as D'Arcy softly whispered: "Oh no…" With the help of Jesus and extensive therapy, I've been able to forgive D'Arcy for that day. But later that evening, while watching the game with Kristina (who didn't know that I knew the outcome) I learned something profound. With our team down by ten points in the final quarter, as Kristina was biting her nails and being taken on an emotional rollercoaster of suspense in the final minutes of the game, my heart was perfectly at rest. Because when you know how the game ends, it doesn't matter what the scoreboard says with two minutes left on the clock.

And when you know how God's story ends, it changes the way we live out our current chapter. And in the pages of our Bible, God has graciously given us a preview of the ultimate outcome of all things. The Author who holds the historical pen has promised a conclusion so gripping, a resolution so potent, a finale so grand and sweeping in its redemption, that on the final day of history as we know it, we will experience, in J.R.R. Tolkien's words, "every sad thing come untrue."

GOD UNDEFEATED, GOD UNDEFEATABLE

God is victorious. To say this is to confess the logical outcome of all the attributes we've explored so far combined. *He cannot lose;* he is undefeated and undefeatable. The victorious God cannot and will not fail in a single one of his purposes. Should the entire created universe rally against him with all its collective fury, it would amount to no more than an army of butterflies waging war against the sun. It's a non-contest. The grand story of human history will climax exactly as God intends it to, and he will be glorified and worshipped and delighted in by his people forever and ever without end. And in the meantime, we have what Peter calls "a living hope" in the character of our God and the certainty of his promises (1 Peter 1:3).

We see such a hope embodied in the life of the apostle Paul. As he neared the final days of his life, he wrote in 2 Timothy 4:16-18 (CSB):

At my first defense, no one stood by me, but everyone deserted me. May it not be counted against them. But the Lord stood with me and strengthened me, so that I might fully preach the word and all the Gentiles might hear it. So I was rescued from the lion's mouth. The Lord will rescue me from every evil work and will bring me safely into his heavenly kingdom. To him be the glory forever and ever! Amen.

Paul is writing from a Roman prison (again), merely weeks or months away from having his head removed from his body. Yet hear the confident hope in his tone! "The Lord *will* rescue me … and will bring me safely into his heavenly kingdom" (v 18). Paul didn't know how the exact circumstances of his own story were going to end; but he did know how God's story was going to end. His hope was not in his physical deliverance but in the God of deliverance who would surely accomplish his purposes in Paul's life, as well as Paul's death. And when we likewise become convinced that God is undefeatable—when we become certain that how God has declared his story will end is exactly what is going to take place—we too can press on with living hope in our living Saviour. In Christ you have a future that nothing in this world can give you and nothing in this world can take away from you. Death can't even scratch you. Because if you are alive in Christ, your future is life everlasting. Your future is *resurrection*.

JESUS RESURRECTED, JESUS RETURNING

Why was Paul not haunted by death? Where did he find the power to confess that for him "to live is Christ, and to die is gain" (Philippians 1:21)? Here's where: in the irrevocable conviction that Jesus had risen. As he wrote to another church, "If Christ has not been raised, your faith is futile and you are still in your sins" (1 Corinthians 15:17). In light of the words and life and death of Jesus, the most important

ADAM RAMSEY

question in the world we could ever consider is: *did he really rise from the dead, like he said he would?*

If there was no resurrection, then the payment Jesus made as the sacrifice for our sins was rejected.

If there was no resurrection, then the whole Bible was written by liars or lunatics.

If there was no resurrection, then there is no hope.

And yet the empty tomb guarded by trained military soldiers bears witness that Christ was raised in victory (Matthew 27:62 – 28:15).

And the hundreds of eyewitnesses—including his own brothers—bear witness that Christ was raised in victory (1 Corinthians 15:5-8).

And the explosive growth of the church in the very place of his crucifixion bears witness that Christ was raised (Acts 2:41-47). There was no passing of generations where myths could develop, nor relocation to a new city where lies could creep in. The only viable explanation for thousands upon thousands of people becoming followers of a crucified Saviour—under the threat of persecution themselves—in the same city where the events took place, is the resurrection.

And the transformation of Saul, a persecutor of Christians, into Paul, a leader of Christians—willing to follow Jesus through beatings, shipwrecks, prison and eventually his own martyrdom—can only be explained by the truth that Christ was indeed raised in victory! For on a dusty road heading toward Damascus, Paul was intercepted by the risen and victorious Jesus. And he was never the same again. The resurrection changes everything, and everything in Christianity hinges on the resurrection.

Are we really so surprised? Jesus himself called his own game-winning shot well before the first Easter weekend. In John 11:25-26, immediately before he raised three-days-dead Lazarus out of his grave, Jesus said:

I am the resurrection and the life. Whoever believes in me, though he die, yet shall he live, and everyone who lives and believes in me shall never die.

Jesus is risen, therefore Christianity, from beginning to end, is resurrection. The moment Jesus opened his eyes and inhaled his first resurrection breath, death received a taste of itself. The second that Jesus got up out of the grave, he validated every one of his claims to be God. His promises are true. His victory is irreversible. His resurrection, for all who place their lives in his hands, turns death from a grim-reaper into a gain-giver. Is it any wonder that Christians, more than all others, are a people of *hope*? The new life we receive at salvation from our risen Saviour, by the regenerating power of the Holy Spirit, is the reason Paul says that we are now "heirs according to the hope of eternal life" (Titus 3:7).

Yet not only did our Saviour rise in triumph, he promised he would return. There is a day on God's calendar in our shared future, where Jesus will indeed split the sky and return in a blaze of glory just like he said he would. He will come as the one true King of kings and Lord of lords, with fire in his eyes and crowns upon his head, striking the final blow against all evil with no more effort than a word from his mouth (Revelation 19:11-16). No one from that moment forward into eternity-future will ever question who reigns as the undisputed champion of the universe. On that day, every knee will hit the dust and every tongue will confess his glory (Philippians 2:10-11). But right now, between the *Hallelujah!* ("Praise God") of Christ's resurrection, and the *Maranatha!* ("Come, our Lord") of his promised return, we learn to wait with patient hope.

LIVING BETWEEN "ALREADY" AND "NOT YET"
Essential to a healthy Christianity is understanding the tension of what theologians call "already" but "not yet." In

Jesus, the kingdom of God has come but is also still yet to come. Heaven has broken into earth through a virgin's womb, but we are still yet to see heaven-on-earth in the way Revelation 21 describes it. When Peter says that we have been "born again to a living hope through the resurrection of Jesus Christ from the dead" (1 Peter 1:3), that word "hope" implies the existence of something that is longed for but yet to be.

This is why the type of false teaching known as "the prosperity gospel" is so destructive; it promises Christians the totality of their inheritance in Christ right now, missing the point that this glorious inheritance is being "kept in heaven for you, who by God's power are being guarded through faith for a salvation ready to be revealed in the last time" (1 Peter 1:4-5). Millions of people around the world are regularly sold the lie that worldly wealth or success are guaranteed if you just believe hard enough; and the crushing disappointment that inevitably follows when it doesn't materialise vandalises the biblical vision of God's faithfulness.

But God never promised his children perpetual prosperity in this present age. On the contrary, Jesus promised us troubles in this world, even if he has indeed overcome the world (John 16:33). Trials in this life are all part of the plan. So we shouldn't be surprised when suffering turns up on our doorstep like an unwelcome enemy soldier billeting at our home (1 Peter 1:6-7; 4:12-13). That is the reality of life in the already-but-not-yet.

Right now, we get a preview, not the whole movie.

Right now, we get a foretaste, not the eternal feast.

Right now, we who have received the Spirit share in the cosmic groaning of creation that is longing for its complete and final liberation from the curse of sin.

There are many spiritual realities that only make sense when viewed through this vital biblical lens of already-but-not-yet. For example, in one sense we have already been adopted in God's family (Romans 8:15), but in another sense we have not yet received the fullness of it since we still "wait eagerly for adoption as sons" (Romans 8:23). Families who have had a foster care situation turn into an adoption know this tension in a profound way, as they await the final court approval for a child who has already become a part of their family. In the same way, in Christ we become part of God's family, but the full experience of that wonderful reality won't be realised until we are finally home with him forever. Living in the tension of promises-given and promises-fulfilled is normal Christianity.

WAITING WITH HOPE

Paul goes on in Romans 8 to apply the tension of our already-but-not-yet reality to our experience of hope. He reminds us that hope belongs to the realm of the future. In verses 24-25 he writes:

> *For in this hope we were saved. Now hope that is seen is not hope. For who hopes for what he sees? But if we hope for what we do not see, we wait for it with patience.*

Our English word for "hope" is admittedly a fairly weak one. When we use it, it's usually in the context of *wishing* for something to happen that we're not totally convinced will. We *hope* our lives go according to plan, but we know that life can throw a mean curveball. We *hope* we don't get sick, but there's no guarantee. Yet biblically speaking, hope goes far deeper than good vibes or nervous optimism. Biblical hope is a confident anticipation that is grounded in the character and promises of God. Ours is a *living hope*, because ours is a *living Saviour*.

Like the moments before being reunited with a loved one.
Like a song right before the beat drops.
Like the sun's rising.

We know exactly what's coming—because we've been given a peek into the final page of God's great story.

I remember hearing someone once put it like this. Imagine you're on a battlefield, and there's one final hill to take. The fighting has been fierce, the enemy has been cunning, and the blood has been real. Suddenly a call comes in over the radio: long range missiles with pinpoint accuracy have been launched and will obliterate every last shred of that final enemy hill ahead of you in eight minutes time. What do you have now? You have hope; a confident anticipation. You know exactly what's coming. And though for eight more minutes the fight rages on; for eight more minutes you experience long seconds that feel like eternity; you know the final battle has been won. You may still take a bullet in the process, yet victory is certain. It's just a matter of time. That's what it feels like to live with a living hope.

Our hope is a helmet that guards our minds against worry over our futures (1 Thessalonians 5:8). Our hope is a north star, that shines with guiding brightness when the night is blackest. Our hope is a sunrise that chases away the darkness every morning. Our hope, in the words of theologian Michael Bird, is currency for when we are passing through the land of melancholy.[55] And that's because our hope is anchored to Jesus the Risen One. He is the Light that the darkness could not overcome (John 1:4-5); he is the Voice that chases away death and despair; he is the Promise of God to you in the present, that crushes all of Satan's lies about your future.

The reason we can take heart is because our hope is not in ourselves but in a God who specialises in resurrection. And he wants us to remember that the resurrection of Jesus not only has cosmic implications for the glorified future his people will share with all of creation (Romans 8:19-22), but personal implications that will energise us in the midst of our struggles today.

10 BILLION YEARS FROM NOW...

Think with me about a definite moment in your distant future. Think of your ten billionth anniversary in glory. There you are, standing with Jesus, looking squarely into his eyes, no longer "in a mirror dimly, but ... face to face" (1 Corinthians 13:12). In that future moment, you will experience an affection from him and a glory in him so dazzling, that as you try to recall the worst moment of your short earthly existence or the most difficult situation you faced in his service, you will say, "I don't even know how to compare the two!"

You will be in the longed-for rest of the new creation where God will dwell with his people (Revelation 21:1-5). You will be standing in the felt reality of the risen King who will wipe away every tear from your eyes and where "death shall be no more, neither shall there be mourning, nor crying, nor pain anymore, for the former things have passed away" (v 4). And there, in the fullness of resurrection life that will never diminish, there will be no more cancer or depression, no more emergency rooms or children's hospitals, no more SWAT teams or security screens, no more wars or funerals or hatred or sin. Our faithful God—seated victoriously on his throne—declares to you now with certainty from your definite future, "Behold, I *am* making all things new" (v 5, emphasis added).

It is here, in this glorious promise, that the battle-tired and life-weary can take heart! There is coming a day where every painful thing will be in the rear view, while unending beauty and newness lie in front of you. There is coming a day of such victorious finality, that the worst of your sins and sufferings will have no more power over your eternal joy than a bad dream you had as a five-year-old has power over you now.

There will not be a single person in the new creation who will ever wonder, "Was it all really worth it?"

In light of Christ's victory, we can face the days ahead with confident anticipation. While we may not know the exact path forward, we do know the Guide, along with the promises of what he has prepared for us. And it's more glorious than we could ever imagine. There is coming a day where our gospel will no longer be news we announce but a song that we sing and a story that we retell. So onward we stumble, for we know how this story ends. In light of *who* God is and *what* he has won on our behalf, let's gladly embrace any cost that comes our way now. Sooner than we think, the clock will run out, and the final page will be turned. Sooner than we think, we will be embraced by glory. Sooner than we think, we will behold him face to face. And we will find ourselves at the beginning of the real story, like the Pevensie children of C.S. Lewis' novels, who discovered...

> all their life in this world and all their adventures in Narnia had only been the cover and the title page: now at last they were beginning Chapter One of the Great Story which no one on earth has read: which goes on forever: in which every chapter is better than the one before.[56]

In Christ, that's where you're heading. And if God cannot lose then neither, beloved Christian, can you.

REFLECTING AND APPLYING

1. In light of the resurrection of Jesus from the grave, what are some ways Christian hope is different to mere optimism or wishfulness?

2. How does knowing that God cannot lose change the way you embrace tensions and disappointments?

3. If you can, think forward to a moment with Jesus ten billion years from now. How does that future conclusion with him empower you to live with confident anticipation in the present page of your life?

Reformation And Revival

"There cannot be true revival unless there has been reformation, and reformation is incomplete without revival. May we be those who know the reality of both."
FRANCIS SCHAEFFER

Thinking rightly and feeling deeply. My goal in this book has been to help us do both; to paint a biblical picture of God that opens our hearts in song. To show him as he is, so that we can enjoy him as he desires us to. I am convinced that God does not want us to settle for theological precision about him that is absent of an ongoing, felt-experience with him. Right thinking is our hearth; right experience is the flame. Why should we pursue anything less than a Christianity that is marked by both biblical thinking *and* spiritual intensity?

Blaise Pascal, one of the intellectual giants of the past thousand years, knew that both were possible. As a renowned philosopher, mathematician, and physicist, Pascal was no stranger to deep thoughts about God and the world he lived in. But nor was he a stranger to the presence of God. After he died, a diary section of an experience he'd had with God was discovered, sewn inside his favourite coat. This experience was so important to him that he literally wore the description of it as a daily reminder to himself of the sheer joy of knowing God's nearness. Here's what this French super-genius had written down:

In the year of grace 1654, Monday, 23rd November,
the day of St. Clement ... From about half-past ten in
the evening until about half an hour after midnight,
FIRE! God of Abraham, God of Isaac, God of Jacob,
not of the philosophers and of the learned. Certainty.
Joy. Certainty. Emotion. Sight. Joy. Forgetfulness of the
world and all outside of God. He is only found in the
ways taught by the gospel. Grandeur of the human soul.
Righteous Father, the world has not known you, but
now I have known you. Joy! Joy! Joy! Tears of joy.

And on and on like this the note goes. A supernatural,
experiential, Spirit-led Christianity and a studying, intellectual,
Bible-soaked Christianity need not be at odds with one
another. In fact, I'd go even further: they must not be.

More than ever before, we need what the author Richard
Lovelace called, "Spirit-empowered biblical thinking."[57] The
kind of Christianity that refuses to settle for either lifeless
orthodoxy or lively foolishness. So I return a final time to
some questions I asked at the very beginning. What if we
Christians of the 21st century were known for a faith that
was as intelligent as it was passionate? What if deep thoughts
about God and deep experiences of God became the norm
for our worship in every area of our lives? Or to frame it even
more robustly: what if we gave the rest of our lives to pursuing
both *reformation* and *revival*?

There is rarely a day that goes by where the words of
Francis Schaeffer at the top of this chapter do not haunt me
in the best of ways. I so want that: reformation *and* revival.
Pure doctrine *and* a Spirit-filled life. Schaeffer reminds us
that the concepts of reformation and revival are not enemies
that stand in contrast with one another, but friends that
dwell together in sacred, life-restoring unity. In his own
words he writes:

Reformation speaks of a restoration to pure doctrine, revival of a restoration in the Christian's life. Reformation speaks of a return to the teachings of Scripture, revival of a life brought into proper relationship to the Holy Spirit.[58]

Here's the point: we should never pit one against the other. We always need both. Indeed, it is our holy privilege to spend our lives seeking both. Do you long for this? Do you long for *him*? In light of *who* this God is—something we've barely scratched the surface of in these pages—I want to invite you to join me on the road of a *living theology*. I want you to close this book and commit yourself anew to continually gazing at God—through both the highs and lows of life inevitably coming your way—until your heart learns to sing in every circumstance. I want you to stubbornly decide that you will never again settle for either right thinking or right feeling. Jesus calls us to follow him into a passionate orthodoxy that sees him truly and enjoys him daily. This book began with a foreword from one of my friends and heroes, Ray Ortlund. And it seems fitting to let him have the final exhortation, as we press forward into all that God desires for us:

[It is] God [who] stimulates in our hearts a longing for him ... [and] that yearning he is awakening in you is the most important thing about you. It's the key to your future. Fan that flame, and never let it die.[59]

Acknowledgements

There are so many to whom I owe a debt of gratitude for the way they have shaped my life, and therefore the words of this book. But I am particularly thankful to the following people (and inanimate objects) that helped bring this work together:

Coffee, I know how many writers forget to acknowledge you. Thank you, friend. You're the real hero here.

Tony Merida, I hold you responsible for pushing me over the edge, through your constant and generous encouragement, in taking the writing side of my ministry more seriously. Thank you, brother.

Alex Early, ditto on the above, and also for telling me that my first title idea was nerdy and dumb (which was true). Your friendship, example, and infectious love for Jesus bleeds through these pages.

Rachel Jones (and The Good Book Company), for your patient, thorough, and insightful edits that sharpened the message we hope to bring to readers.

Tearna Reid, for being the most tremendous assistant; you give cohesion to the craziness, and synergise the various spheres of my life—including this book—into liveable rhythms.

Ray Ortlund, for not only coining the term, but embodying the reality of "gospel-beast." Your impact is immeasurable; I'm beyond grateful for your wisdom, friendship, kindness, and example, along with your brilliant foreword!

Laura Haas, Arnaldo Santiago, and Léonce Crump for your refreshingly honest feedback on various chapters and ideas during the early stages of writing.

The people of Liberti Church for the privilege of being your pastor and teaching you the Bible; I love so much what God has done in us these past (almost) seven years.

Brad and Hilary Ramsey, my parents, for instilling in me a hunger for books from the earliest years of my life and for loving our family so selflessly.

And most importantly, to my wife Kristina: your voice and influence comes through these pages more than you know. I treasure those nights of reading drafts together, your brilliant edits and tweaks, along with our occasional grammar-battle. And though we may never see eye-to-eye on the (obvious) superiority of the hyphen and em dash—those glorious, idea-fusing treasures of the punctuation world—I am grateful for you, my love, most of all.

To God be all the glory.

Endnotes

1 Brennan Manning, *Abba's Child: The Cry of the Heart for Intimate Belonging* (Navpress, 2015), p 155.

2 Aiden Wilson Tozer, *The Knowledge of the Holy* (Authentic Media, 2016), p 1.

3 Jen Wilkin, *Women of the Word: How to Study the Bible with our Hearts and our Minds* (Crossway, 2014), p 31.

4 C.S. Lewis, *The Silver Chair* (William Collins Sons & Co, 1980), p 26-27.

5 Aiden Wilson Tozer, *The Knowledge of the Holy* (Authentic Media, 2008), p 91.

6 Eugene Peterson, *Eat This Book: A Conversation in the Art of Spiritual Reading* (Hodder & Stoughton, 2006), p 69.

7 Corrie ten Boom, *The Hiding Place* (Hodder & Stoughton, 2001), p 194-195.

8 I heard this mic-drop summary of this story, from Ray Ortlund in a sermon on Psalm 23, https://www.immanuelnashville.com/resources/multimedia/details?id=1657308 (accessed May 7, 2020).

9 Arthur W. Pink, *The Attributes of God* (Baker Book Company, 2008), p 41.

10 James D. Bratt (ed), *Abraham Kuyper: A Centennial Reader* (Eerdmans, 1998), p 488.

11 John Piper, *John G. Paton: You Will Be Eaten by Cannibals!* (Desiring God Foundation, 2012), p 22.

12 C.S. Lewis, *Mere Christianity* (Harper Collins, 2001) p 124.

13 Dane Ortlund, *Edwards on the Christian Life: Alive to the Beauty of God* (Crossway, 2014), p 72.

14 J.W. Bready, *England: Before and After Wesley* (Hodder & Stoughton, 1939), p 229.

15 J.I. Packer & Carolyn Nystrom, *Praying: Finding our Way Through Duty to Delight* (Intervarsity Press, 2006), p 175.

16 Francis Schaeffer, *The Complete Works of Francis Schaeffer: Volume 3* (Crossway Books, 1982), p 44.

17 Aiden Wilson Tozer, *The Knowledge of the Holy* (Authentic Media, 2008), p 97.

18 Sam Storms, "The Omnipresence of God", https://www.samstorms.org/all-articles/post/the-omnipresence-of-god/ (accessed July 11, 2020).

19 Scott Sauls, *Jesus Outside the Lines* (Tyndale House Publishers, 2015), p 101.

20 J.D. Greear, *Gospel: Recovering the Power That Made Christianity Revolutionary* (B&H Publishing, 2011), p 56.

21 Dane Ortlund, *Gentle and Lowly: The Heart of Christ for Sinners and Sufferers* (Crossway, 2020), p 83.

22 Ray Ortlund, "Suffer and Rejoice: Start Now to Finish Well in Ministry", https://www.thegospelcoalition.org/conference_media/suffer-rejoice-start-now-finish-well-ministry/ (accessed June 18, 2020).

23 Alex Early, *The Reckless Love of God: Experiencing the Personal, Passionate Heart of the Gospel* (Bethany House, 2015), p 66.

24 Jen Wilkin, *In His Image: 10 Ways God Calls us to Reflect His Character* (Crossway, 2018), p 48.

25 Brennan Manning, *Ruthless Trust: The Ragamuffin's Path to God* (HarperCollins, 2000), p 178.

26 Notes recorded by the author during a session at the Acts29 Pastors Retreat in Long Beach, California (July 26, 2016).

27 Shel Silverstein, *The Giving Tree* (HarperCollins, 1964).

28 C.S. Lewis, *The Collected Letters of C.S. Lewis, Volume 3* (HarperCollins, 2007), p 119.

29 Reynolds Price, *Letter to a Man in the Fire* (Scribner, 1999), p 54.

30 Timothy Keller, *King's Cross* (Hodder & Stoughton, 2011), p 9.

31 Frederick Lehman, https://hymnary.org/text/the_love_of_ god_is_greater_far (accessed July 20, 2020).

32 Roger E. Olsen, https://www.patheos.com/blogs/ rogereolson/2013/01/did-karl-barth-really-say-jesus-loves-me-this-i-know/ (accessed July 20, 2020).

33 D. M. Lloyd-Jones, *Romans: An Exposition of Chapters 7.1-8.4* (Edinburgh, 1973), p 61.

34 Jen Wilkin, *None Like Him: 10 Ways God is Different From Us (and Why That's a Good Thing)* (Crossway, 2016), p 71.

35 C.S. Lewis, *Yours, Jack: Spiritual Direction from C.S. Lewis* (HarperCollins, 2008), p 97-98.

36 Alan Kreider, *The Patient Ferment of the Early Church: The Improbable Rise of Christianity in the Roman Empire* (Baker Academic, 2016), p 1.

37 Tertullian, "Apology", in *Ante-Nicene Christian Library, vol. 11, The Writings of Tertullian: Volume I*, trans. Alexander Roberts and James Donaldson (T. & T. Clark, 1869), p 119.

38 Victor Hugo, *Les Misérables: Volume 1* (Collins Clear Type Press, 1920), p 57-88.

39 Aiden Wilson Tozer, *The Knowledge of the Holy* (Authentic Media, 2008), p 117.

40 Scott Sauls, *A Gentle Answer: Our 'Secret Weapon' in an Age of Us Against Them* (Thomas Nelson, 2020), p 18.

41 Richard Sibbes, *The Bruised Reed and Smoking Flax* (Banner of Truth, 1998), p 13.

42 Dane Ortlund, *Edwards on the Christian Life: Alive to the Beauty of God* (Crossway, 2014), p 91.

43 Herman Bavinck, *Reformed Dogmatics: God and Creation, Volume 2* (Baker Academic, 2004), p 222-224.

44 Fleming Rutledge, *The Crucifixion: Understanding the Death of Jesus Christ* (Eerdmans, 2015), p 130.

45 Scott Sauls, *Jesus Outside the Lines: A Way Forward for Those Who Are Tired of Taking Sides* (Tyndale House, 2015), p 111.

46 Scott Sauls, https://scottsauls.com/blog/2020/06/06/i-thought-i-was-opposing-racism/, (accessed June 28, 2020).

47 Eric Mason, *Woke Church: An Urgent Call for Christians in America to Confront Racism and Injustice* (Moody Publishers, 2018), p 32.

48 James Burns, *The Laws of Revival* (Calvary Chapel Philadelphia, 2013), p 71-72.

49 Randy Alcorn, *Does God Want Us to Be Happy?: The Case for Biblical Happiness* (Tyndale Momentum, 2019), p 13.

50 John Piper, *Seeing and Savoring Jesus Christ* (Crossway, 2006), p 36.

51 Augustine, *The Confessions of St Augustine* (Spire Books, 2008), p 161.

52 Martyn Lloyd-Jones, *Authentic Christianity: Studies in the Book of Acts, Volume 1* (Crossway, 2000), p 177.

53 George Müller, https://www.georgemuller.org/devotional/the-first-great-and-primary-business (accessed January 29, 2021).

54 Alcorn, *Does God Want Us to Be Happy?*, p 168.

55 Michael Bird, *Romans: The Story of God Bible Commentary* (HarperCollins, 2016), p 288.

56 C.S. Lewis, *The Last Battle* (Lions, 1956), p 172.

57 Richard Lovelace, *Dynamics of Spiritual Life: An Evangelical Theology of Renewal* (Paternoster Press, 1979), p 281.

58 Francis Schaeffer, *No Little People* (Crossway, 2003), p 74.

59 Raymond C. Ortlund Jr., *Isaiah: God Saves Sinners* (Crossway, 2012), p 147.

thegoodbook
COMPANY

BIBLICAL | RELEVANT | ACCESSIBLE

At The Good Book Company, we are dedicated to helping Christians and local churches grow. We believe that God's growth process always starts with hearing clearly what he has said to us through his timeless word—the Bible.

Ever since we opened our doors in 1991, we have been striving to produce Bible-based resources that bring glory to God. We have grown to become an international provider of user-friendly resources to the Christian community, with believers of all backgrounds and denominations using our books, Bible studies, devotionals, evangelistic resources, and DVD-based courses.

We want to equip ordinary Christians to live for Christ day by day, and churches to grow in their knowledge of God, their love for one another, and the effectiveness of their outreach.

Call us for a discussion of your needs or visit one of our local websites for more information on the resources and services we provide.

Your friends at The Good Book Company

thegoodbook.com | thegoodbook.co.uk
thegoodbook.com.au | thegoodbook.co.nz
thegoodbook.co.in